C0-AMV-370

Library of
Davidson College

VOID

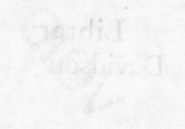

GREEKS AND LATINS ON CYPRUS

GREEKS and LATINS on CYPRUS

IN THE THIRTEENTH CENTURY

by

Miltiades B. Efthimiou

HELLENIC COLLEGE PRESS
Brookline, Massachusetts 02146

956.45
E27g

© 1987 by Hellenic College Press
Published by Hellenic College Press
50 Goddard Avenue
Brookline, Massachusetts 02146

All rights reserved.

Cover and jacket design by Mary C. Vaporis

Library of Congress Cataloging-in-Publication Data

Efthimiou, Miltiades B.
Greeks and Latins on Cyprus.

Bibliography: p.
Includes index.
1. Cyprus—Church history. 2. Orthodox Eastern Church—
Relations—Catholic Church. 3. Catholic Church—Relations—
Orthodox Eastern Church. 4. Cyprus (Archdiocese)—Relations—
Catholic Church. 5. Catholic Church—Relations—Cyprus (Arch-
diocese). 6. Cyprus (Archdiocese)—History. 7. Catholic Church—
Cyprus—History. 8. Cyprus—History. 9. Kingdom of God—
History of doctrines—Middle Ages, 600-1500. I. Title.
ISBN 0-917653-27-0
ISBN 0-917653-28-9 (pbk.)

95-8883
ACE-4953

To
PATRIARCH ATHENAGORAS

and
FATHER BASIL
who taught me Godliness,

and
ARCHBISHOP IAKOVOS

and
MY MOTHER, HELEN
who continue to teach me. . .

Hellenic College Press wishes to acknowledge
with thanks the generosity of the men listed below
whose contributions made possible the publication of
Greeks and Latins on Cyprus in the Thirteenth Century.

STEVE ALEXANDER
ANDREW ATHENS
DR. ANTHONY BORDEN
NICK BOURAS
MICHAEL CANTONIS
ALEC P. COURTELIS
MICHAEL JAHARIS
GEORGE LIVANOS
HARRY MAGAFAN
JOHN L. MARKS
GEORGE PARASKEVAIDES
ANGELO TSAKOPOULOS
MIKIS THEODOSIOU

Contents

LIST OF PHOTOGRAPHS AND MAP

Map: page 16. Important sites of thirteenth-century Cyprus.

1. Kolossi Castle: dates from the 15th century B.C.

2. Machairas Monastery: about 26 miles south of Nicosia dating from the 12th century A.D.

3. The Monastery of Apostolos Andreas (Apostle Andrew): at the extreme eastern tip of the island — Cape Andreas — 11th century.

4. Kyrenia

5. The Monastery of St. John Chrysostomos: situated on the southern slope of Kyrenia range and built in A.D. 1090.

6. Othello's Tower: served as the citadel of Famagusta built by the Lusignans and later on remodelled by the Venetians in 1492.

7. St. Hilarion Castle: the summer residence of the Lusignan Kings of Cyprus. The name of the castle is attributed to St. Hilarion the Great, a 6th century Syrian hermit and a friend of St. Jerome. During the 10th century the Byzantines built a church here and then a monastery in memory of St. Hilarion. During the Lusignan reign, it was adapted as a Catholic establishment and later converted into a fortified castle in 1228.

8. Monastery of Stavrovouni: the first buildings of the monastery and church were built by order of St. Helena, the mother of Constantine in A.D. 327. According to tradition, St. Helena gave a portion of the holy Cross to the monastery, hence its name.

9. Bellapais Abbey: the most remarkable Gothic monument in Cyprus, the 13th century "Abbey of Peace," is situated in a small Kyrenia mountain village of the same name.

10. Kykko Monastery: the largest and most famous monastery in Cyprus. Founded in A.D. 1100 in the reign of the Byzantine Emperor Alexios Komnenos. He gave it an icon of the Virgin Mary with the Child, believed to have been painted by St. Luke.

11. Hagia Napa Monastery: Hagia Napa village takes its name from the ancient Greek Orthodox Monastery of Hagia Napa located in the village, 14th-15th century.

12. The Monastery of Apostolos Barnabas: St. Barnabas is the patron saint and founder of the autocephalous Greek Orthodox Church of Cyprus. The monastery is situated one mile west of Salamis, near Famagusta.

13. The Monastery of Saint Neophytos the Recluse: founded by St. Neophytos in A.D. 1159.

14. The Giuliana Gate, now the Famagusta Gate: this gate, due east, was the strongest, most elaborate, and principal gate of the city, named in honor of Count Giulio Savorgnano, who built the city walls in 1567.

15. View of the left ear of the d' Avila bastion. The Town Hall, the main post office and the Public Library are situated on this bastion. A part of the city wall is seen on the right of the picture, the row of Palm trees. The walls around Nicosia were built by the Venetians (1567-1570).

Photos courtesy of Mr. K. Psyllides — Director, Press and Information Office, Republic of Cyprus.

INTRODUCTION

The following chapters attempt to interpret the meaning and spirit of Orthodox Christianity as a movement which finds its center in the faith — in the kingdom of God. What is in these pages shows a distinct pattern, which clearly indicates that the movement is complex: moreover, it can be suggested only vaguely and in outline. Hence it may be of some help to the reader if the author reveals why he undertook this study, what problems he sought to solve, and what general conclusions he reached.

Throughout my studies at Holy Cross Theological School, and subsequently at Boston University and Miami University of Ohio, and even in my work in various parishes of the Greek Orthodox Archdiocese of North and South America as well as with the handicapped and underprivileged persons that I worked with, I sought to discover the nature of the relation of religion to people. The study of Cyprus in the Middle Ages is really a reflection of these personal concerns on an academic plain, where one sees people through the eyes of two opposing cultural and ecclesiastical forces. In Cyprus, these forces were reflected in patterns of race, ethnicity, religious persuasions, and sectional interests as they manifested themselves in the two very ancient branches of Christendom. Examining the ecclesiastical, doctrinal, political and religious differences with points of contention between Byzantines and Latins, we are able to see why the religious stream flowed in particular channels, as well as the unity which Christianity possesses despite its varities. Religion was dependent on the respective traditions, thus giving us a faith which is independent, which is agressive rather than passive, and which molds tradition instead of being molded by it. Furthermore, the only answer I was able to give to the problem of Christian disunity was in the form of a widespread and loosely connected appeal for what is good and enabled the Church to overcome stubborn social, cultural and ecclesiastical divisions and to make incarnate the ideal of Our Lord and Savior Jesus Christ. This appeal seemed, upon critical reflection, to have been wholly inadequate, especially on the part of the Western foreign invader.

The pursuit of these and related problems led me to renew my study of Orthodox Christianity in and throughout the Byzantine East, although it was only as an amateur, as one who feels the need of testing the abstract ideas of ecclesiology and ethics in the laboratory of history, that I was able to pursue this study, and continue to do so in my present position as Director of the Department of Church and Society, dealing with daily social and moral concerns for the Greek Orthodox Church. At first it seemed likely that the various decretals such as the *Bulla Cypria* or the *Partitio Romaniae,* which played so great a role in Cypriot religious thought and practice in the history of the island, might offer a clue to the central intention, the common interest, and the independent force of the papacy. If many Roman Catholic historians could deal with the ethics of Catholicism despite its great variety, by tracing the idea of the vision of God through early and mediaeval Cypriot history, might it not be possible to use the idea of papal understanding of the kingdom on earth in a similar fashion for understanding and interpreting Byzantine Christianity, and from this vantage point to be able to discern a unity in religion which was hidden to the eternal view? To some this idea seemed closely related to that "mystical reality" which V. Lossky had used so effectively in interpreting man's vision of God.

The expectation of the Latin West and Byzantine East was the great common element in traditional faith, and by reference to it one might be able to understand not only the underlying unity and the diversity of these two Christian churches, but also the effect of Christianity on culture and ethnicity. This expectation might be the heart, the unyielding core which kept religion from becoming a mere function of culture; which enables it to recover its initiative, to protest as well as to acquiesce, to construct new orders of life on Cyprus as well as to sanctify established orders; which accounted for its relenting position, explained its relations to the autocratic, Caesaropapist attitudes and its creativity in producing even more of an Orthodox fervor among the dissident populace.

In other words, it was simply impossible to force Cypriot Greeks, inheritors of the great Byzantine tradition, and the great leaders of the thirteenth and fourteenth century into the mold of Western, legal, and papist thought. In them a "vis-a-tergo" rather than the attraction of an ideal seemed to be the motivating force. The Western crusaders and dynasties who landed in Cyprus had a profound influence on the Cypriots, but it was not wholly negative, for it appeared that the foreigners did not seek to actually and totally dominate the populace. They became intimately related to the social and ecclesiastical faith of the Cypriots. What the relationships were and the unity obtained in the whole process became clearer to me as I brought the insights of historians like Steven Runciman, Robert Wolff, and Dionysios Zakythenos, with their great studies of static and dynamic theocracies, and of John La Monte, V. Laurent, and many other contemporary thinkers to bear on the subject. In consequence, I was led to certain discoveries in the field of thirteenth-century Christianity.

The first theme was that the kingdom of God had indeed been the dominant idea in Western and Eastern Christianity — just as the "vision of God" had been paramount in mediaeval faith — though it had not always meant the same thing. The Kingdom of God, relative to Cyprus, at times meant "sovereignty of God" and the "reign of Christ," so that each complemented the other, and without each the Kingdom would be incomplete.

This is the theme of this work; it is a theme which could not be developed in a single chapter and the scope of the

appears only as the whole book is taken into account. This may
seem to be an effort to present theology in the guise of history,
yet the theology of the interaction between East and West in
the period after the Schism has grown out of history as much
as history has grown out of the theology.

I would like to underscore some convictions which this study
has fostered. First, it fostered the conviction that Christianity
as received from the Apostles and passed down to the Fathers
of the Church, and reflected in historical evolution, both in
mediaeval Cyprus and America, must be understood as a movement rather than as an institution or series of institutions. Christianity is Gospel; it is *Evangelion* rather than law, being more
dynamic than static. The genius of Christianity does not appear
in ethical programs, in chrysobulls or decretals any more than
its various creeds, important as they may be at times; these are
pronouncements from the Church's life and become lifeless sym-
bols when they are utilized as ends in themselves. The true
Church of Christ is "one, holy, catholic and apostolic" and
because it is an organic movement of those who have been "called
out" and "sent," the saints, the martyrs, the ascetics, and the
hierarchs show what Christianity is. Since the goal of Christianity
is the infinite and eternal God, only movement or life directed
towards the ever Transcendent can express its meaning.

A second conviction is closely connected with the first.
Christianity as a movement cannot be represented in terms
of simple progress in either an other-worldly or a this-worldly
direction, nor can it be stated only in terms of canons and rules
which always imply a static view. The relation of God to the
world which is infinitely dependent upon him, but which nevertheless seeks to travel an independent way, to a foreign world
which remains the object of his redeeming love, requires of
those who seek to be obedient to the divine imperative a dialectical movement. This dialect is expressed in liturgical worship
and in efforts directed toward God, as well as towards the
world which loved God and whose efforts constantly are to
make his will a reality on earth. It is impossible to express the
Christianity of the Fathers in terms of a one-way movement

toward the infinite and eternal God who draws men to himself, for this God so loved the world that he gave his only-begotten Son for the world's salvation. It is equally impossible to express it in terms of love of the creature alone, for the meaning of the creature does not lie in itself but only in God. The life of the Church, as well as the life of Christian individuals, illustrates this dialectical process; a study of the Latin and Orthodox churches, so close in time to the schism of 1054, illustrates this as much as any other. The evil habit of humans to criticize their predecessors for having seen only half of the truth hides from them their own partiality and incompleteness. Thought and faith remain in a fragmentary state; only the object is one. A true understanding of mediaeval Christianity in the East and in the West, as they interacted at a point of time in history on the island of Cyprus, does not seek a synthesis in which the dialectic can come to rest; only God can provide this synthesis. Yet this understanding does its proper work in its own time and with full recognition of the partial character of its interest, combined with full faith in the whole organic life which makes the partial work significant. The beauty of studying Eastern and Western Christianity during this period of time is due not only to the fact that no one church or group of Christians can represent the universal but also that no one time, only all times together, can set forth the full meaning of the movement toward the Eternal and his created image. One of the great needs of present day institutionalized and divided Christianity is recovery of the faith of the "one, holy, catholic, and apostolic Church." The study of the dialectic character and the continuity of the Christian Byzantine East with the Latin West is one aid to such a recovery. It helps us to tolerate, understand, and love those who express a phase of Christian history other than that which our own church expresses; it warns us of our own limitations, yet encourages us to do and seek his will with all our might; it entices us to seek unity, not on the level of hazy sentimentalism, but on the level of the active intellectual, moral, ecclesiastical, and religious conflict of those who contend truthfully because they share a common faith in God.

A final conviction taken from the study of thirteenth century Cyprus is that true Christianity cannot be understood except on the basis of faith in a sovereign, living, and loving God. Apart from God, the whole interpretation of history is meaningless and might as well not have existed. Apart from God and his forgiveness, culture, language, tradition, and even Christianity particularized in east and west, north and south, become destructive rather than creative. The history of mediaeval Cyprus, of the interaction between Greek East and Latin West, leads one to the history of the Kingdom of God. Hence, my greatest hope is that this book may serve as a stepping stone to the work of new generations bringing final peace to the island of Cyprus, whose paradigm comes from that time when the paralysis of two opposing forces of the East and the West seemed quite evident in this small, insignificant, yet godly island and whose signs were never lacking of a new spirit stirring from among the old forms. May this be unto Cyprus a new recovery of faith of those past ideals of the past which were indications of an indomitable spirit that in time became the seed plot of new life.

The research, planning, and writing of this book is the result of gathering information for my dissertation and from the various opportunities for travel over the years. For this opportunity and for the continued encouragement and advice I am indebted to His Eminence Iakovos, Archbishop of North and South America, and to the late Ecumenical Patriarch of Constantinople, Athenagoras I. Those who knew the kindness and magnitude of Athenagoras will understand how deeply I regret that this work could not have been published before he died. I am dedicating this work to him, as well as to my late father Basil, and my mother Helen whose prayers continue to be a source of inner strength for me.

A work of this kind necessarily owes much to those who have written about Cyprus in the past. The names of the many scholars, from whose writings I have freely and gratefully drawn, appear in the bibliography. However, I must recover here my respect for the memory of Sir George Hill, whose pioneer work on Cyprus — three volumes published in the 1940s — formed the point of departure for my own research.

Other support and assistance has come from many quarters. Miami University of Ohio, the University of Cincinnati, the University of Dayton, and St. Leonard's College at Centerville in Ohio, Dumbarton Oaks, Harvard University, Fordham University, Hellenic College, as well as numerous other libraries and archives in the United States and in Europe offered me associations that contributed much to my research. The Vatican Library in Rome, the Pontifical Institute in Rome, the University of Athens, the Cyprus Museum in Nicosia, the Department of Antiquities on Cyprus, and the Greek-Cypriot, the Turkish-Cypriot and the United Nations information officers in Nicosia were all invaluable sources of information. The late Dr. Porphyrios Diakaios, professor of archaeology and mediaeval studies at Heidelberg University and former director of the Cyprus Department of Antiquities, spared no effort helping and guiding me in the use of manuscripts, photostats and provided me with a particularly helpful research program at churches and monasteries in Cyprus.

Many friends, associates, colleagues, and teachers have helped in many ways, and to all these I offer humble thanks. To the professors of history at Miami University, Oxford, Ohio, professors of history, especially to Dr. Richard Jellisson and Dr. Herbert L. Oerter under whose guidance the work for my doctoral thesis was commenced and finished, I can never sufficiently express my gratitude. I am also indebted to Dr. Harry J. Magoulias of the Department of History, Wayne State University of Detroit, Michigan, for his guidance and advice. Thanks also to Kiki Demetrion, Dolores Revelos, Pearl Vradelis of Middletown, Ohio and Efthimia Meimaroglou of Athens, Greece. Finally, I thank Fr. N. Michael Vaporis, whose generosity and assistance brought this work to fruition. I need not empasize that I alone am responsible for any deficiencies in this book.

Miltiades G. Efthimiou
New York City, 1986

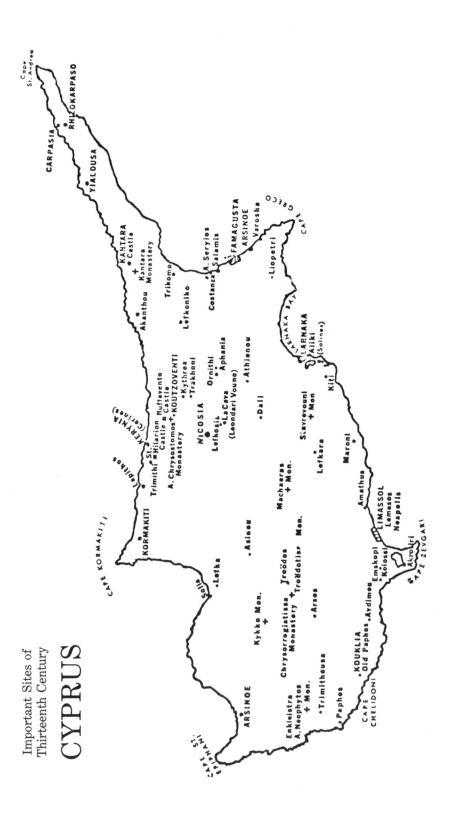

Important Sites of
Thirteenth Century
CYPRUS

Cape
St. Andrea

RHIZOKARPASO

CARPASIA

YIALOUSA

CAPE GRECO

KANTARA
Castle
Kantara Monastery

Akanthou

Trikomo

Lefkoniko

FAMAGUSTA
Varosha
ARSINOE
A. Serios
Costanza Salamis
Lliopetri

LARNAKA BAY

LARNAKA
Ailiki
(Salines)

Kiti

Lefkara

St. Hilarion Castle
Ruftavento Castle
A. Chrysostomos Monastery
KOUTZOVENTI
Kythrea
Trakhoni
Ornithi
Aphania
La Cava
(Leondari Vouno)
KERYNIA (Cerines)

Lapithos

KERYNIA
(Cerines)

Trimithi

NICOSIA
Lefkosia

Dali

Athienou

Stavrovouni
+ Mon.

Maroni

Machaeras
+ Mon.

Amathus

LIMASSOL
Lemesos
Neapolis

CAPE KORMAKITI

Solia

KORMAKITI

Lefka

Asinou

Kykko Mon.
+

Chrysorrogiatissa
Monastery + Troödos Troödotis. Mon.

Arsos

Emskopi
Kolossi
Akrotiri
CAPE ZEVGARI

ARSINOE

Enkleistra
A. Neophytos
+ Mon.

Trimithusa

Paphos

KOUKLIA
Old Paphos Avdimou
CAPE CHELIDONI

CAPE ST.
EPIPHANI

Chapter One

CYPRUS PRIOR TO THE FOURTH CRUSADE

The Latin conquest of the Byzantine East gave rise to a particular concept of rapprochement which belongs specifically to the Latin West. However, the concept contributed more than just a little to religious hatred between these two halves of the Christian world. The movement east was neither a popular migration, a war of conquest undertaken by an ambitious monarch, nor a search for new colonies and trade routes, though all these elements were present in the crusades to a comparatively minor degree. Whether one agrees with Nicholas Iorga that the conquest of Cyprus was an integral part of Richard I's grand strategy for his crusade, or with George Hill that the conquest was only a "side issue," which later developed into a major operation, the Latin foreigners and other adverturers before them had arrived on Cyprus with the firm intention of staying and keeping possession of all conquered land.[1] They did not feel that they were destroying an established order or depriving a land of its independence or its inhabitants of their country. By virtue of the Orthodox separation from Rome, the idea of a Christian kingdom of Cyprus, prolonging or restoring Latin supremacy in the East, was not incongruous in itself, nor was the migration east considered an arbitrary undertaking for motives of conquest and pillage. The conquest of Cyprus rested, according to the West, on

17

lawful grounds. The land to which the foreigners came had been so torn and ravaged that their appearance might well have proved, as many Cypriots hoped, a force for order. In any event, the Latin empire of Constantinople, the Latin kingdom of Cyprus, and other Latin states in the East had already compromised this hope.

During the earliest years of their establishment in Cyprus, the crusaders — or at least those who chose to remain in Cyprus and so were no longer, properly speaking, crusaders — showed neither curiosity nor tolerance at being confronted with a new way of life, another civilization, and peoples whose race and religious practices were alien to their own. They were too preoccupied with the urgent business of keeping their place in the land by either converting the Cypriots or defending their land. At times differences of language and customs did not prevent them from understanding one another and especially from reaching agreements to further their own interests. Their religious antagonism remained insoluble. The Latins were trying to create in this new land a province of their own in the image of the West. They were remarkable builders of churches and castles. The building frenzy which had overrun Europe at the end of the eleventh and through the thirteenth century reappeared in Cyprus on a scale that is surprising when one remembers the small density of the Latin population. Of course, many Christian churches existed, and they restored these in the Latin mold. The foreigners, however, possessed the ambition to build new churches and to embellish and enlarge those already existing, in addition to erecting private houses, convents and monasteries, country houses, and above all, castles. Therefore, the Latin kingdom of Cyprus was actually a country governed by a Western aristocracy, which was a class controlling the land, the government of the cities, the administration of justice and finance, and, most important of all, the religion of its native inhabitants.

ORGANIZATION

At the head of this aristocracy was the king, or, in the major fiefs, the counts or barons. As in the West, the king's personal domain was small, usually around Nicosia. The remainder of the kingdom was distributed in fiefs to the major vassals, who in turn had vassals of their own. As in the West, all feudal lords, great and small, drew their wealth in principle from the land entrusted to their care. Actually this land did not produce enough. Although the coast, the valley near Lapithos and Karavas, and the southern flank of Pentadaktylos near Kythrea were fertile provinces, the central plain, the Mesaria, the Pedias, and Gialias areas were on the whole poor. The income from the land was often inadequate and the barons often supplemented it with various taxes such as road tolls, customs' dues, and levies on contracts for buying and selling. Peasants and churches were compelled to pay a capitation tax greater than the produce of the land which they had to give to their lord. The king presided over the council of barons and the courts of justice and appointed men to the highest offices. Yet, the government of the kingdom was, theoretically, in the hands of a *Haute Cour,* a High Court. As the principal administrator of the property of the state, the king was empowered to distribute fiefs, which were taken from his personal domains. He could also prevent his vassals, as well as the Church, from selling their domains if the proposed sale seemed to him damaging to the interests of the kingdom.

Consequently, feudal society — namely, the king, his major vassals, and their vassals — lived its own life, somewhat cut off from the rest of the population, very much as it did in the West. Relationships between feudal society and the people were similar to those between the Western nobility and the peasants. The Cypriots seemed foreign to the Latin and Frankish barons.

THE FATE OF THE INDIGENOUS CYPRIOT

Prior to the Fourth Crusade, no Greek or Syrian author left memoirs or a chronicle dealing with the rule of the crusaders in the East. Byzantine historians from Constantinople, Asia Minor or Cyprus generally ignored events in Cyprus and Syria and dealt mainly with the Empire's western policies and the wars with the Seljuks. Only Anna Komnene mentioned the crusades. She saw the crusades as a disturbing, interesting, even amazing phenomenon of minor importance. Quite naturally, many Byzantines witnessed the Fourth Crusade. The Holy Land, Jerusalem, or the Empire's interests in Palestine no longer concerned the Fourth Crusade. Events proved that Anna Komnene was right. This entire barbarian drive toward the East was simply a different aspect of one vast enterprise aimed at the destruction of the Eastern Roman Empire. The Greeks believed that the Christian crusaders were more dangerous than any Muslim. This opinion was not entirely unfounded, if one considers events in their historical perspective. Like every great empire, Byzantium regarded itself as the center of the world, the only really civilized country, the guardian of truth in matters of religion and the heir of Roman greatness, Greek thought, and Christian revelation. Naturally the Empire set up the care of its own interests as a moral right. A Greek would not have conceived the expression "Byzantine perfidy." The proudest of totalitarian states in our own day could never equal Byzantium in its calm awareness of its own sovereign rights and its ineradicable consciousness of superiority. This attitude was largely a religious feeling, because the Church was a state church and the emperor was the secular head of the Church. Byzantium was not exactly a theocracy, but the intent was to unite the theocratic ideal of Judaism to the absolutism of Rome mingled with reminiscences of Oriental despotism. Even when they were harried on all fronts, losing province after province, constantly in the grip of economic crisis and on the edge of collapse, the rulers of Constantinople still behaved like masters of the world. The Byzantine aristocracy attached more importance to court intrigues and quarrels between factions which split the capital than to battles being waged by their armies on the frontiers of the Empire.

During the reign of Heraklios (610-41), the Semitic tribes of Arabia swept over the tax-ridden, heretical and already Semiticized southern provinces of the Byzantine Empire. In

639, Mu'awiya, chief of the Quraish, Muhammad's own clan, destined to be the founder of the Umayyad dynasty, became emir of Syria. With the consent of the caliph Othman, he planned to attack Cyprus and, using the newly-captured naval base at Alexandria, outfitted a fleet of 1700 ships.[2] This endeavor was the first Arab maritime enterprise on any scale. Between 648 and 649 Mu'awiya landed on Cyprus and sacked Konstantia, massacring most of its inhabitants and dividing the spoils with his allies from Egypt. He filled seventy of his ships with the proceeds and imposed an annual tribute of 7,200 pieces on the Cypriots. When the Cypriots failed to pay the annual tribute, in 653 Mu'awiya sent another force under Abu'l-Awar, which massacred more of the inhabitants and stormed their refuge at Lapethos. He reimposed the tribute and left behind an Arab garrison of 12,000. Others who followed Mu'awiya in subjecting the island were Caliph 'Abdal-Malik (685-705), Omar II (717-720), Hishan (724-743), and the Abbasid Mansur (754-775).

During the time that Cyprus was subjected to the cruelties of an oppressor, attempts were made to revitalize the Empire. In the frontier provinces a warrior class was trained to free Cyprus. These warriors were celebrated in the later Akritic cycle of heroic poems. The hero of the cycle, Digenes Akritas, also lived in Cypriot folklore. A rock near the southwest coast, where Aphrodite emerged from the rich and creamy-like foam of the seas, bears the name, "Petra tou Romiou." The story is that Digenes hurled this rock at the Saracens when they called him "Romios," a pejorative term for a Greek. Other stories of Digenes, kept continuously alive by Greek ballad singers, associate him with the Troödos and Kyrenia Mountains. In the twentieth century, when the late George Grivas began guerilla campaigns in those very mountains, he assumed the name of Digenis.[3]

The latter half of the seventh century was an unfortunate time for the Cypriots, and their culture suffered as a result. Because the Arabs destroyed the basilica at Konstantia, the headquarters of the Cypriot primate was transferred to nearby

Arsinoe Ammochostos (Famagusta), where it remained until the Latins transferred the primacy to Nicosia toward the end of the twelfth century.[4] In the sixth year of Constantine V's reign as emperor of Constantinople (747), two events ocurred: bubonic plague took the lives of many Cypriots and the caliph Mervan II from Alexandria sent a fleet of 1000 dromonds (large, swift ships) against Cyprus. The Muslims suffered a humiliating defeat by the Kibyrrhaiot theme, the military command centered on the Pamphylian coast. During the eighth century at the time of the Isaurian dynasty, Cyprus continued to be a place of exile for undesirables, and in 770 monks and nuns at Ephesos who were not given permission to marry by decree of the emperor of Constantinople, were sent to Cyprus in exile.[5] In 773 a Muslim fleet carried off the governor of the island, and under the leadership of Caliph Harum ar-Rashid (786-809), two expeditions ravaged Cyprus. In 806 the *Wali* of the Syrian coast carried off many captives including the bishop of Cyprus. Basil the Macedonian (867-86) made Cyprus a theme of the Empire. His general, Alexios the Armenian, governed the theme for seven years only, when an Arab fleet under the admiral Dimyana plundered Cyprus for four months.[6] After Nikephoros Phokas was crowned emperor of Byzantium in 964 and especially from the time following his successor, John Tzimiskes, the position of the clergy on the island was strengthened and Cyprus enjoyed a period of relative peace.

By the end of the Arab invasions, the following cities no longer existed and remained in history only as names on the map: Konstantia, Amathos, Tamassos, Soli, Karpasia, and Kourion. Kition was transferred from its site near Larnaka to a village farther south. The ancient city of Lapethos became the village of Lapithos. The inhabitants of the port of New Paphos took refuge in Ktema on the low plateau along the coast. The principal cities that emerged to form a new page in the history of Cyprus were Ammochostos (Famagusta), Lefkosia (Nikosia), Lemesos (Limassol), and Kyrenia (Kerynia).

From the second half of the tenth to the first half of the

twelfth centuries, peace reigned on the island. During this time, one finds a revival of Greek Cypriot Christian art. In the eleventh century the textile industry flourished, and the prosperity of the island accordingly increased. Monasteries, too, prospered. The great monastery at Kykko was built under the patronage of Emperor Alexios Komnenos. Other monasteries of the time include Mahairas in the central hills and those of Trooditissa and Chrysirryiatissa, which took the place of destroyed monasteries like Arakas and Asinou.

The country was beautiful, though too barren in some regions and too hot for men who came from Normandy, Flanders, and elsewhere in the thirteenth century. However, the coastal plains, the plain of Mesaria, and the foothills of Mt. Troödos were so providentially fertile that men could gather three harvests in one year and grow not only corn, vines, and apples, but also other fruits, such as oranges and lemons, unknown in Europe, and many varieties of vegetables and sugar cane. The forests of the highlands and the foothills near Mount Boukasa in the Troödos range produced the finest woods for building and were all stocked with game. As good landowners, the Latins and Franks prized all this productivity. They appreciated and admired the comforts and beauty of the cities. The superb fortifications and defense works excited them so much that they began covering the land with castles, romantic fortresses on the crest of the mountain ranges in the north — St. Hilarion, Buffavento, and Kantra. A man could love this land with its wooded hills, calm white villages, cypress groves, stony tracks where donkeys passed laden with stone jars and baskets of olives, broad roads along which the caravans traveled, deep blue skies, and cold, starry nights. From this land Latin and Frankish foreigners effortlessly gained their wealth from the spoils of victories that others had achieved before them. They had come east and simply had more opportunity of exercising their trade in the East than in Europe, where conquest had long since become a public scourge. They could subjugate with clear conscience because the Church, far from condemning their pillaging as fatricidal, proclaimed them agreeable to God. They also acquired comparatively more profit since the rights of pillages were more loosely applied in lands owned by schismatic brethren.

The story of thirteenth-century Cyprus begins at this point with the arrival of a feudal nobility and the arrival of a military machine. By profession the nobles were a caste of soldiers who could feel confortable in the country. Because of their training, their sole aim was the subjugation of this alien people. The time of the great invasions had passed. Even the struggles against the Moors in Spain and Slavonic and Lithuanian pagans in the north of Germany had become merely spasmodic local outbreaks. The Norman advance had ceased to be a menace to the West. No longer could the West drive back a powerful aggressor or conquer new lands. The West was discovering its own internal balance. This discovery was, admittedly, precarious. Not too long before, bitter struggles had developed between pope and emperor for the domination of Italy and Byzantium. Uprisings among the great feudal lords in Germany and the great vassals of the French crown and quarrels between Saxons and Normans in England occurred. These controversies could not prevent Europe from gradually becoming a collection of peoples belonging to one civilization, the product of Western feudalism and the Roman Catholic religion. The feudal system was the life and soul of this new civilization, but feudal society was essentially warlike and subjugated less fortunate people. The West no longer offered sufficient scope for subjugation and overthrow. The apostasy of the East offered the perfect substitute for new horizons based on old ideals.

1. Kolossi Castle — 15th century

2. Machairas Monastery — 12th century

Chapter Two

CYPRUS IN THE
THIRTEENTH CENTURY

While Constantinople provided a new outlet for Western adventurers, the kingdom of Cyprus was growing prosperous. The island, an area of 3584 square miles, emerged into history when Thotmose III of Egypt conquered it in 1500 B.C. The culture of the island at that time was Mycenaean with a cult of Aphrodite situated at Paphos. The Phoenicians later built trading posts there. In 58 B.C. Rome annexed Cyprus, and Cicero became administrator of the island for one year. From the fourth century until 1191, Cyprus was an outpost of the Byzantine Empire, Greek-speaking and Byzantine in its culture. The Arabs raided the island repeatedly. The crusaders from Antioch and Tripoli also raided Cyprus. In 1191, when the ruler Isaak Komnenos, an unpopular tyrant, attempted to abduct Berengaria, the betrothed of Richard I, and Richard's sister, Joan of Sicily, the English King conquered the island, sent Isaak as a prisoner to Syria, and sold Cyprus to the Templars. They apparently could not manage the affairs of the island and returned it to Richard, who installed Guy of Lusignan as administrator. Guy had helped Richard to conquer the island. This event marked the establishment of the most successful Latin dynastic state in the eastern Mediterranean.

The Lusignan dynasty, which governed Cyprus from 1192 until 1369, played an important part in the history of thirteenth-century England. Guy's father was Count Hugh VIII, called "le Brun." His namesake and successor, Hugh X, count of La Marche, became the second husband of Isabella of Angouleme, who had been queen of England and the wife of King John. King Henry III maintained a hold in central France through the support of his stepfather, "whose widespread and loosely connected lands sprawled across parts of seven modern departments from the upper valley of the Creuse to the east and of the Vienne to the north of Limoges through Lusignan to his castles in Poitou." [1]

The three hundred years during which kings and queens of this family ruled Cyprus included the most brilliant epochs in the island's dramatic history. Influenced greatly by the Latin empire of Constantinople, the constitution of Cyprus was a model of the feudal state. The *Assizes of Jerusalem* embodies the laws of the constitution of Cyprus. Politically and socially the Lusignan kingdom, however, great as it was, if regarded solely from the Frankish standpoint, meant the subjection of the native peasantry, Greek-speaking and Orthodox, to a French-speaking, Roman Catholic feudal aristocracy from the West. Ecclesiastically the policy of the Lusignans and the popes followed parallel lines: this policy subordinated the autocephalous Orthodox Church to the church of the ruler. The Latins endowed the Latin sees with property taken from the Orthodox bishoprics; a series of acts of oppression culminated in 1260 in the issue of the *Bulla Cypria* by Pope Alexander IV, in which the Latin archbishop became the supreme ecclesiastical leader of both Latins and Orthodox alike. The Latin clergy received all tithes; the Orthodox archbishopric was suppressed, and the Latins obligated the Orthodox bishops to take the oath of obedience to the Latin bishops.

The establishment of a Latin kingdom in Cyprus gave certain advantages to the crusaders of the thirteenth century. Protected by the surrounding seas, the island became an ideal retreat for crusaders, for whom "the possession of Cyprus allowed them to prolong for another century their occupation of the Syrian seaports." [2] After 1291 planners of future crusades still looked to Cyprus as their advance base, but the emphasis among crusaders and churchmen changed from crusading zeal and ecclesiastical reform to lust for commercial profit.

A study of the Latin empire of Constantinople and of the kingdom of Cyprus offers to the historian an opportunity to see the deterioration of relations between the Latin West and the Greek East at a time when the Eastern Empire was already in decline and dependent upon the Latin West for its own defense. This historical fact should not surprise anyone inasmuch as the position and resources of the island eventually involved the island in the destiny of the crusaders either in the Levant or in Anatolia. One need only look at the map of mediaeval Cyprus (see map) to notice that Cape Andreas, the easternmost tip of the island, lies only a day's sail from the coast of Syria, less than seventy miles away; the northern coast of the island is forty miles from the coast of Anatolia. For centuries Cyprus was a way-station for pilgrim traffic to the Holy Land. Since the time of the First Crusade, Cyprus intermittently provided ships and supplies to the crusaders but at the same time had friendly relations with the Muslims. In 1148, the Emperor Manuel Komnenos granted commercial privileges in Crete and Cyprus to the Venetians. His decision indicated that the western powers were increasingly penetrating Cyprus. This concession, so full of consequences for the future, came when Manuel was seeking the alliance of the Venetians against the Normans who had captured the island of Corfu.[3] In 1155 or 1156 a French adventurer, Renaud de Chatillon, married to Constance, princess of Antioch, launched an expedition against Cyprus. The invaders burned towns and churches, mutilated the inhabitants (both lay and clergy), took gold, pillaged and performed a "criminal rape" of the island, according to William of Tyre.[4] He reasoned that the pillaging might have been justifiable if Christian had fought against Muslim, for this was the age of the crusades and the Latin kingdoms in the Holy Land.[5]

Numerous precedents existed for Renaud's attacks against

Cyprus. Shortly after the schism between the Greek and Latin churches in 1054, Anna Komnene reported that an insurrection had occurred in Cyprus and Crete.[6] The insurrection involved two chieftains, Karykes in Crete and Rhapsomates in Cyprus. Emperor Alexios Komnenos dispatched his brother-in-law Doukas, the recently appointed grand duke of the imperial fleet, who put an end to the revolts. Having killed Karykes, the Cretans handed Crete over to Doukas, who left the garrison to oversee the island while he went to Cyprus. When he landed, Doukas took Kerynia by assault, captured the island with his commanding general, Michael Boutoumites, and imprisoned Rhapsomates. The emperor then designated Kalliparios judge and assessor of taxes for the island of Cyprus and sent him there. Eumathios Philokales received the military command of the island. The emperor appointed him "stratopedarch" and gave him warships and cavalry. Philokales repelled Bohemond when that crusader landed on Cyprus in 1099. Aided by a Pisan fleet dispatched by Daimbert, archbishop of Pisa, Bohemond attacked Laodicea on the Syrian coast. The Laodiceans soundly defeated Bohemond, and the remaining vessels marauded the islands in the Mediterranean. The forces of Philokales immediately destroyed those landing on Cyprus and dispersed the army.

Prior to the coming of Renaud de Chatillon in 1155, the first half of the twelfth century passed peacefully for the most part. Sir George Hill, whose monumental four-volume work, *A History of Cyprus,* remains the classic in the field, cites certain pertinent events affecting the external politics of the island.[7]

1. Erik the Good of Denmark visited the island during the period. He died of fever at Paphos on July 10, 1103, before reaching the Holy Land. He was buried at the cathedral near the present church of Chrysopolitissa.

2. Relations with the Muslims were good. When Baldwin captured Beirut on May 13, 1110, the Muslim emir fled by night to Cyprus. Inhabitants of Beirut who also sought to flee the oppression transported the Muslims' possessions to the island.[8]

3. In 1123 the doge of Venice, Domenigo Michiel, came to Cyprus on his expedition against the Muslims. Although Venice was unfriendly to the emperor of Byzantium at this time, no historical evidence exists of any damage done on Cyprus.[9]

4.The influx of Maronites, a monotheletic Christian sect, into the island is evident. Maronite patriarchs elevated two monks (in 1121 and 1141 respectively) to abbot of the monastery of St John Chrysostom at Koutzoventi.[10]

5. In 1136, Emperor John II Komnenos removed the Armenian population of Tell Hamdun in Little Armenia to Cyprus.

6. In 1142, the emperor conceived a plan to unite Cilicia, upper Syria, and Cyprus into one state. Had the plan been effectuated, it would have had far-reaching implications connected with the approaching threat of Latin penetration into Cyprus. John II Komnenos proposed a hereditary principality in favor of his son Manuel. Hill agrees with Chalandon and other authorities[11] that this decision really meant reconstituting the ancient duchy of Antioch and placing his son in command. The plan apparently failed.

The arrival of Richard I, king of England, enhanced the groundwork for further Western penetration. Richard encountered Isaak Doukas Komnenos, the "tyrant" of Cyprus from 1185-1191, who was an enemy of the Latins and an ally of Saladin.[12] The events leading up to Richard's coming to Cyprus are rather familiar, and no disagreement exists among scholars. Richard of England and Philip II Augustus of France embarked on the crusade but circumstances held them up at Messina in 1190. They decided to spend the winter there. Richard was betrothed to Alice, the sister of Philip. This engagement ended shortly thereafter when Richard became betrothed to Berengeria of Navarre.

On April 10 Richard's fleet sailed. A storm separated the ships. Those ships carrying Berengeria and Richard's sister, Joan of Sicily, eventually found their way to Lemesos on Cyprus. Isaak ordered the Cypriots to prevent the crusaders from touching any port of the island. He brutally treated or held as hostages those who escaped from the wrecked ships off Lemesos. Isaak attempted, however, to entice Joan and Berengeria to land so that he might hold them for ransom. Suspecting Isaak's plan, they refused and stayed on the wrecked ship off shore waiting for Richard. On May 6, 1191, Richard landed on Cyprus. Within one month Richard had conquered the island and had married princess Berengeria.[13] They had met on Sicily when Eleanor of Aquitaine had brought the princess with her.[14] The conquest of Cyprus was a very profitable venture. The conquest rid the island of Isaak, who had seized control of Cyprus from Constantinople in 1184 with the help of his brother-in-law, the Sicilian admiral Margarit. This event occurred before Isaak Angelos had overthrown Andronikos Komnenos at Constantinople (1185) and had seized the imperial throne. The English chroniclers present Isaak as a villain who refused to send supplies to the Christians in Palestine and who robbed pilgrims who came to his shores. In addition to taking treasures in battle, Richard levied a heavy tax on the island. Meanwhile, Isaak had retreated to Lefkosia and had sent his wife and daughter for safety to the castle of Kerynia.[15] Richard now sent his army along the coast as far as Kiti (Larnaka) to avoid penetrating the hilly country; from there he continued to Famagusta. Philip sent envoys to Richard at Famagusta telling him to hurry to Acre. Richard's reply was that Cyprus was too important a commercial center to leave. He then marched toward Lefkosia. At a place called Tremethoussia, the two armies met. According to one account, the engagement was fierce and ended when Richard overwhelmed Isaak. Another account mentions that the encounter was a skirmish. Isaak escaped to Kantara or took refuge in the Parpass near Cape Andreas. At Lefkosia Richard became ill. Guy de Lusignan, a lord from Syria who had joined Richard along with sixty other knights, besieged Kerynia, which surrendered; Isaak's wife and daughter fell into Richard's hands. Isaak, learning of his family's capture, negotiated a surrender of the island to Richard. Richard agreed not to put him in irons. When Richard departed, he left a small garrison under the command of Richard de Camville and Robert of Turnham. On June

5, 1191, he set sail for Acre.[16]

From this point the history of Cyprus takes an interesting turn. The present investigation concentrates on this turn of events which climaxed in the rational "cuius regio eius religio." The French kings were content with a policy of toleration. They wanted to maintain peace and order in their dominions. However, the conversion of the Greeks persistently interested the Latin Church. During this period the Roman pontiff vacillated in his policy toward the Greek Orthodox people. At times the Latin Church viewed the Greeks as heretics and subjected them to persecution and force; at other times the Latin Church viewed them as schismatics and treated them with moderation and toleration.

When Guy de Lusignan died at the age of sixty-five in April of 1194 after a reign of only one year and eleven months in Cyprus, his brother and successor Aimery obtained in 1197 from Emperor Henry VI a royal crown which entitled him to be called "Constable of Jerusalem and King of Cyprus."[17] His first task was to straighten out the financial problems that Guy's generous donations had left to beset the kingdom. Aimery succeeded in persuading his vassals and knights to restore to him the lands and fiefs which were now worth twice as much as they has been when Guy had been alive.[18] Aimery attempted the attainment of two goals: to make his kingdom solvent and to make it Latin Catholic. Although Latin clergy and monks had previously arrived with crusaders, Aimery's charge to the archdeacon of Laodicea was to offset the recalcitrant Greek clergy by the presence of the Latin Church.[19] Pope Celestine III ordered the archdeacon of Laodicea and Aimery's chancellor Alan, archdeacon of Lydda, to organize the Latin church of Cyprus.[20] These two delegates of the pope organized Cyprus into an archdiocese with three suffragan dioceses.[21] Alan became archbishop of the Cathedral Chapter of Nicosia. The pope chose the archdeacon of Laodicea for the see of Paphos. The identity of the first bishops of the other two Latin sees is unknown. However, in a bull dated December 13, 1196, the pope laid down rules and regulations for each diocese and for numbers of the religious orders. The bull intended to return the island and its inhabitants, in the pope's words, to the bosom of the Roman Church from which they had separated.[22] The bull noted above, or any other document of this period including Gams (see note 22 below), does not mention the relationship between the Latin archbishop of Cyprus and the other Latin patriarchates of the East. In fact, rather than do homage to anyone else, Aimery obviously decided to ask for the crown from Henry VI, who was planning a crusade and who was only too willing to see Cyprus as his fief. Henry sent the royal sceptre to Aimery in custody of the bishops of Trani and Brindisi. The imperial chancellor, the bishop of Hildesheim, who led the expedition, was to conduct the coronation.[23] In addition to these insults, the Latin patriarch of Jerusalem, now residing in Acre, began sending delegates to make periodical visits to Cyprus. These incidents terminated the ancient privilege of automomy under Byzantine rule.

The Thirty-ninth Canon of the Quinisext Synod of 692 A.D., a continuation of the Sixth Ecumenical Synod, ratified by the Seventh Ecumenical Synod, reads as follows:

> Since our brother and fellow-worker, John, *proedros* of the island of Cyprus, together with his people in the province of the Hellespont, both on account of barbarian incursions, and (in order) that they may be freed from servitude to the heathen and may be subject alone to the sceptres of most Christian rule, has emigrated from the said island, by the providence of the philanthropic God, and the labor of our Christ-loving and pious Empress; we determine that the privileges which were conceded by the divine fathers who first at Ephesos assembled, are to be preserved without any innovations, viz. that New Justinianopolis[25] shall have the rights of Constantinople and whoever is constituted the pious and most religious bishop thereof shall take precedence of all bishops of the province of the Hellespont, and be *elected* by his own bishops according to ancient

custom. For the customs which were obtained in each church, our divine fathers also took pains that they should be maintained, the existing city of Kyzikos being subject to the metropolitan of the aforesaid Justinianopolis, for the limitation of all the rest of the bishops who are under the beloved of God Metropolitan John, by whom, as custom demands, even the bishop of the very city of Kyzikos shall be ordained.[26]

According to this canon, the church of Kyzikos, as defined, is that of an autocephalous church subject to no superior ecclesiastical authority, a status preserved prior to and subsequent to the Lusignan dynasty. The third Ecumenical Synod at Ephesos in 431 accorded privileges to the church of Cyprus. Canon Eight embodies these privileges:

. . . The Rulers (bishops) of the holy churches in Cyprus shall enjoy, without dispute or injury, according to the canons of the blessed Fathers and ancient custom, the right of performing for themselves the ordination of their excellent Bishops.[27]

Some fifty years later, about A.D. 480, the patriarch of Antioch, Peter the Fuller, questioned the autocephaly of the Cypriot Church. According to tradition, the timely intervention of the Apostle Barnabas, founder of the church of Cyprus, thwarted Antioch's claims. Barnabas allegedly appeared to Anthemios, the archbishop of the island at the time, in a dream and indicated to him the proper course of action. Accordingly, Archbishop Anthemios went in solemn procession to the place indicated in the alleged dream and discovered the Apostle's tomb in which he also found a copy of Matthew's Gospel which the Apostle himself had transcribed.[28] The archbishop then proceeded to Constantinople and presented the Gospel to the Emperor Zeno. On the advice of a local synod, Zeno accepted the Cypriot claim to independence in ecclesiastical matters because Cyprus was just as much an apostolic foundation

as Antioch, the first see of Peter. Thus the archbishop confirmed the autocephaly of the Cypriot Church; in addition, the
emperor granted the archbishop the right to sign in red ink
— a distinction till then enjoyed only by the emperor — and
the right to wear a purple cloak at church festivals and to carry
and imperial sceptre instead of a pastoral staff.[29] The archbishop of Cyprus has retained these privileges, expressing
recognition of temporal authority, to the present day. After
the Fourth Crusade, Rome tried to place Cyprus under the
Latin patriarchate of Constantinople. Professor Gerasimos
Konidares has recently questioned the full independence of the
Church of Cyprus in the eighth, ninth, tenth centuries and
thereafter.[30] His views may be summed up as follows:

1. Because of the Arab raids against Cyprus, the situation
on the island deteriorated to such an extent that during the
eighth century the whole economic and political life of the
island became absolutely dependent upon that of Constantinople.[31]

2. The Church of Cyprus, unable to manage on its own, had
to ask for the help of the patriarchate of Constantinople; a
closer relationship between the two churches and a gradual
increase in the supervision exercised by the Patriarchate did
not abolish the autocephaly, but before the end of the eighth
century Cyprus became *de facto* a subject of the patriarchate
of Constantinople and its third metropolis.[32]

3. The *de facto* subjection of the Church of Cyprus to that
of Constantinople continued even after the reconquest of the
island from the Arabs by Byzantine forces in the tenth century.[33] A. I. Dikogoropoulos[34] refuted Professor Konidares,
who based his views on the evidence of a number of documents.[35] Dikogoropoulos substantiates that Cyprus retained
the autocephalous status of Canon Thirty-nine of the Quinisext
Synod up to and even during the time of the Latin and French
occupation following the Fourth Crusade. In other words,
Cyprus was not under the jurisdiction of Constantinople. The
"Partitio Romaniae," as well as the chrysobull of Alexios III
drafted in 1199 with Venice, makes no mention of Cyprus and,

thus, is further evidence showing the independence of Cyprus. At the time of the organization of the Latin church of Cyprus, the Greek Church still preserved its fourteen dioceses, its rites and properties. Ecclesiastical organization in Cyprus, as in other parts of the Byzantine Empire, concentrated on cities, each city being the center of a diocese over which a bishop presided.[36] Dikigoropoulos cites, in addition to the metropolis and archiepiscopal residence Konstantia, the following cities of Cyprus: Kition, Amathos, Neapolis, Lemesos, Kyrion, Paphos, Arsinoe, Lapethos, Kerynia, Karpasia, Tamassos, Tremytos, Chytroi, Lefkosia, and Kermeia. Hackett agrees basically with this list of cites and bishoprics.[37] Dikigoropoulos notes that the Church abandoned Neapolis, and Amathos absorbed its see after the Arab raids of the seventh century,[38] while Hill notes that Theodosias or Theodosiana was a temporary name for Neapolis.[39] Some of these cities became insignificant before the end of Byzantine rule (e.g., Kition, Soli — in Hackett's list — Kuriom, Khythir). Others rose to great importance (e.g., Lefkosia [Nikosia], Nemesos [now Limassol], Paphos, Kerynia, Lapithos, Karpasia, Arsinoe, Tremythos). According to the map of the old cities of Cyprus (see map), Chrysochou represents Arsinoe-Marium; Kyrion is now Episkopi; Amathos goes to Nemesos; Tamassos and Chytroi, like Tremithos, come under Lefkosia; Lapithos goes to Kerynia, Avdimou (Evdimou on modern maps), Kilani, Mazotos and the Moraria were agricultural districts.[40]

The revenues received mostly from the public domains or abandoned inheritances supported the Latin Church.[41] All this support for the Latin Church, however, emotionally affected the Greeks. They felt that the foreigners threatened the prestige and the independence of their church and traditions and humbled the religion of their fathers. Yet, when Constantinople fell in 1204 to the French and the Venetians, Pope Innocent III hoped to realize his great dream of the union of the two churches by using a policy of tolerance for the customs, faith and rites of the Greek Church. Three years before the sack of Constantinople, Alexios III appealed to Innocent III.

If the pope would help him to recover Cyprus by excommunicating Aimery, Alexios would give aid to the crusaders. The pope refused, stating that Byzantium had already lost Cyprus when Richard I had conquered it, and the recovery of Jerusalem was most important; hence, it would be undesirable to divert forces of the king of Cyrpus from the crusade to the defense of his kingdom.[42]

The establishment of a Latin kingdom on Cyprus presented certain advantages to the crusaders of the thirteenth century. Cyprus became a central base of operations, where expeditions might meet to launch their planned attacks on Egypt or Syria or to recuperate from the hardships of a long sea voyage.[43]

The occupation of Cyprus, on the other hand, led to certain disadvantages. The island was prosperous and distinctly self-sufficient from early times. Its geographical relation to the mainland offered a distinct advantage over most of the other islands both in the Aegean and Mediterranean seas; the outstretched finger of the Karpass pointed significantly to Syria. This geographical oddity, coupled with the fact that the north coast of the island is about forty miles from that of Cilicia, was an important factor in the thirteenth century. Egypt is farther away. Larnaka is more than 260 miles from Port Said. Relations with Egypt, therefore, did not begin as early as with Anatolia and Syria.[44] Yet, Cyprus proved to be an irrestible attraction not only to the barons of Syria but also to others. Guy de Lusignan and his successors made lands available to foreigners in Cyprus, free from the menace of Muslim raids.[45] The island attracted merchants, and the towns became thriving centers for trade and commerce.[46]

When Guy de Lusignan (1192-1194), ex-king of Jerusalem, purchased Cyprus from King Richard I in 1192, he laid the foundations for the feudal system on the island.[47] The Franks became predominant in church and in state; they reduced well-to-do Cypriots to the class of vassals, and the peasants remained as serfs; Guy's brother and succesor, Aimery (1194-1205), continued the pattern and organized the Latin church of Cyprus with its hierarchy dependent upon the archbishop of Nicosia. He also introduced the feudal code of Jerusalem. Aimery was anxious to establish his authority. He persuaded Henry VI to bestow upon him the title of "King" in 1197 in place of "Lord of Cyprus," borne by his brother.In the following year he added the coveted but empty title of "King of Jerusalem." This double accession, however, proved to be detrimental to the interests of Cyprus. In essence, Western claims to the island led to the subsequent internal strife and diverted Aimery's attention to Syrian affairs.[48] Added to this situation was the appeal of Alexios III to Innocent III in the spring of 1201. If the pope would help him to recover Cyprus by excommunicating Aimery, Alexios would give help and support to the crusaders. The pope refused and Constantinople fell to the Latins, who introduced the feudal system in the East. This feudal system, preserved long after it had crumbled in Constantinople, Epiros, Nikaia, and the Levant, dominated the life of the Cypriot peoples.

In thirteenth-century Cyprus, while new ideas of monarchy were developing elsewhere, the barons attempted to reestablish the old feudal system.[49] By the time Cyprus became a kingdom under the Lusignans, the practice of electing a king had ceased; rule by "hereditary succession" had replaced it. The government still lay in the hands of a *Haute Cour,* or the whole constituency of barons on the island; but the holders of fiefs owed their homage directly to the king and by virtue of this homage were automatic members of the royal court.[50] La Monte further mentions that holders of fiefs who were twenty-five years of age and older were automatically members of the *Haute Cour.* Also included were members of the clergy who had holdings. Special situations arose in which the king granted exceptions or special privileges to important persons who could appear and even preside over the *Haute Cour,* which was responsible for the policy of the king and the direction of the affairs of state. The *Haute Cour* interpreted the old laws and at times created new ones. The *Haute Cour* defended its members against any attack on, or diminution of, their rights.[51] La Monte outlines the official high offices of the kingdom of Cyprus during the thirteenth century: seneschal, constable, marshal, chamberlain and the chancellor.[52] These offices were not hereditary at this time, and the king usually made appointments at his coronation. An official normally held his position for life. Hill explains that the viscount was a local official, corresponding to the English sheriff.[53]

The problem on Cyprus was very obvious at this time: the French ruling class and the native Greek-Cypriots had not amalgamated as had the Normans and the English in England after 1066 and the French and the natives to a lesser extent in Frankish Greece. The inevitable outcome of the establishment of the Latin church was the attempt to convert the Greek Orthodox to Latin Catholicism. In 1211 Wilbrand, count of Oldenburg, son of Henry II, count of Oldenburg, and Beatrix, countess of Hallermund, wrote some rather biased memoirs of the island and its native Greeks:

> The island is extremely fertile and produces excellent wine. It lies near the Cyclades but is not one of them. Its length is four days' journey, its breadth more than two. It has high mountains. There is one archbishop who has three suffragans. These are Latins. But the Greeks, over whom throughout this land the Latins have dominion, have thirteen bishops, of whom one is an archbishop. They all obey the Franks and pay tribute like slaves. Whence you can see that the Franks are the lords of this land, whom the Greeks and Armenians obey as serfs. They are all rude in their habits and shabby in their dress, sacrificing chiefly to their lusts. We shall ascribe this to the wine of that country which provokes to luxury, or rather to those who drink it. It is for this reason that Venus was said to be worshipped in Cyprus . . .for the wines of this island are so thick and rich that they are sometimes specially prepared to be eaten like honey with bread.[54]

To complicate matters further, the Latin clergy ministered largely to the conquerers of Cyprus and their descendants. In the Latin kingdom of Cyprus the Latin aristocracy endowed priests for services.[55] The establishment of the Latin church on Cyprus and the effects of the Latin kingdoms resulting from the Fourth Crusade led to difficulties on two levels. On the one hand, the Latin clergy became involved in misunderstandings with the lay lords and barons whom they constantly accused of not enforcing the collection of tithes on their respective lands as was the custom in the kingdom of Jerusalem. On the other hand — and more important than these differences — the Greek Church, from whom the Latins expected absolute obedience, created the same problems as in Constantinople and the Latin states in the East. The Latin archbishop must be recognized as the metropolitan of all Christians on Cyprus, and the Greek bishops must pay homage and fealty to the Latin bishops.

The Lusignan period began with Guy in 1192 and lost much of its power after the assassination of Peter I in 1369. Relative stability was maintained, despite the rivalry of the Frankish nobles, because society was organized on a hierarchical basis. The period during the thirteenth century was one of great prosperity for the kings and nobles of Cyprus. However, this prosperity was dependent on the ability of the Franks to hold the island by force of arms.

Aimery's heir for the crown of Cyprus was his ten-year-old son by Eschiva, Hugh I (1205-1218). The high court of Nicosia appointed Walter of Mintbéliard, constable of Jerusalem and husband of Hugh's elder sister Burgundia, to the position of both guardian and regent.[56] In 1208, when Hugh attained the marriageable age of fourteen, Walter negotiated the marriage of the young king with Alice, daughter of Henry of Champagne and Isabel of Jerusalem. Hugh's short reign was brought to a close by his death in Tripoli in 1218, while on the Fifth Crusade.[57] He left an heir, Henry I (1218-1253), about eight months old. Henry's mother, Alice, was regent and guardian of the king, even though documents call her "queen of Cyprus."[58] Shortly after Alice was appointed regent, Leopold VI, duke of Austria, made an attempt

Library of
Davidson College

to take over the kingdom, but was foiled by the barons and by Pope Honorius III, who took Alice and the King under his protection. Perhaps as a result of this crisis Alice agreed to associate in the regency with her uncle, Philip d'Ibelin, younger brother of John, the powerful Old Lord of Beirut. In effect, the two d'Ibelins then governed Cyprus.

In 1206 the new Latin patriarch of Constantinople, the Venetian Thomas Morosini, requested the Apostolic See to place Cyprus under his jurisdiction. The pope refused. The representatives of the Roman See proved too often to be tactless, thereby widening the chasm that existed between the Latins and Greeks, especially when they dealt with opponents of a very similar character.[59] The pope could not understand why the Latin rulers of the East were not able to compell, by force if necessary, the recalcitrant Greeks to submit to the Roman Church. He sent them letter after letter reminding them of their obligation to the Church. Soon, however, he decided on a more forceful policy. The pope appointed Pelagius, the bishop of Albano, as papal legate to the East and granted him absolute authority to use any measures necessary to bring about submission of the Greeks to the Apostolic See.[60] Pelagius succeeded only in agitating the Greeks in Constantinople when he closed the Greek churches there and imprisoned the priests and monks.[61] In October 1220, when the Latins were seeking complete control over Cyprus, a council convened at Limassol (Lemesos). The council decided that the Latin Church would receive the tithes on all domain and baronial lands. This act, a custom of the kingdom of Jerusalem, found favor with the queen Alice, the constable, Walter of Caesarea, and the barons of Cyprus on the one side. In addition, Pelagius, the papal legate enforced this act upon Eustorge, Latin archbishop of Nicosia, and the three suffragan bishops of Paphos, Lemesos, and Famagusta. Letters, communicated to the pope by Pelagius and receiving his approval, confirmed the supremacy of the Latin Church.[62] The pope approved the following articles:

1. The Latin Church was to receive tithes on all land belonging

to the crown or the barons in accordance with the usage and customs of the kingdom of Jerusalem.

2. A Latin church was to receive services and dues (*chevagia* and *dimos*) owed to the crown by villeins on estates of the Church. Priests and deacons of the Greek Church were to be free of the *chevagia* and *angaria* (*corvée*) or poll-tax, but the Greek clergy was still required to pay obeisance to the Latin ordinary.

3. Greek priests and deacons were not to move from one *casale* to another, as long as the excess of clergy prevailed.

4. No Greek was to receive ordination without his Latin lord's consent.

5. A Greek ordained outside the island without his lord's knowledge would be punished with suspension of his duties for a period of time. With the consent of his lord, he could return to servitude.

6. No Greek could become a monk or lay brother without his lord's consent.

7. The lord of the area must assent to and the Latin ordinary must confirm the canonical election of Greek abbots; the lord could not remove the abbot from his abbey unless the abbot committed some offence; in all, abbots, and monks would be obedient to the Latin ordinary.

8. Greek churches and monasteries should remain in possession of any benefactions or properties granted them by Latin lords.

9. When Greek priests or deacons moved from one *casale* to another with permission of the Latin ordinary, the lord of the area should appoint other Greeks in their stead.[63]

Pope Honorius implied further control when, in a letter to the queen, the barons and the knights of Cyprus, he directed that the Latin clergy of the island should retain all properties which Greek clergy previously had held. He insisted that the secular leaders and authorities respect these possessions of the Church.[64] Prior to this, Pope Honorius wrote to the patriarch of Jerusalem and the archbishops of Tyre and Caesarea that they should require all Greek bishops to render obedience to the Roman Church in accordance with the agreement between the queen of Cyprus and the prelates of her kingdom.[65] Yet this whole arrangement was distasteful to the queen and her barons. The arrangement was too favorable to the Latin clergy, who were growing in strength and whose lust for power and land was becoming all too apparent. Straining relations further was the stipulation that Greek bishops were to ordain Greek clergy only with the consent of the Latin bishop and temporal lord of the district.[66] In fact the whole situation led to an open break between the queen and her coregent Philip d'Ibelin.[67] At first Philip received exemption from the payment of tithes which before he had paid to the Greeks and now, according to the decision at Lemesos (Articles Two and Eight), paid to the Latin Church. He now found that he would have to pay again, and the queen upheld this decision. Philip and his barons, flatly refusing to pay, defended the Greek priests, saying that the Latin clergy were fleecing them to satisfy their ambitions. Philip reported to the *Haute Cour* that the people hated the Latins who were seditious to the realm and who sold the Eucharist for money, etc.[68] Soon after this the queen left Cyprus for Syria, where she married the heir to the crusader states of Antioch and Tripoli, the future Bohemond V.[69] The important factor affecting all future Greek-Latin relations on Cyprus was that the Latins were willing to permit the Greeks to retain four out of fourteen ancient dioceses on the condition that these titularies should function only under the supervision of the Latin prelate in whose diocese their bishoprics were located.[70] Even though the Latin clergy could not totally convert the Orthodox, they could not leave them without leaders and pastors. The Latin clergy, however, deprived these pastors of all authority and allowed them to exercise their offices only under the supervision of their Latin ordinaries. The Orthodox almost acquiesced to the Latin demands, reasoning that the Latins would do no harm as long as the Orthodox did not violate canons, rites, and traditions of the faith. Two envoys from Cyprus — Leontios, bishop of Soli, and Leontios, abbot of the monastery of Absinthi —

presented to the Ecumenical Patriarch of Constantinople, Manuel I, and to the Holy Synod (now residing in exile in Nikaia) a letter which illustrates their compliance:

Our situation has been up till now very distressing, but we were able, however, to bear our misfortunes, because only our bodies had to suffer the tyranny of the Franks. Today our souls also are threatened: the voice of the Holy Church is about to be choked. Together with the Latins, some priests of the same race have come to the island and have subverted our churches, invaded our domains, and placed a sacreligious hand on things divine. Our lawful pastor, the most blessed archbishop of the Cypriots, Neophytos, exiled from his see, has been replaced by a stranger, inexperienced, and taken from among the Latins. This man wants our bishops and priests to make submission by placing their hands in those of the Latin bishops, before having the right to govern and teach the faithful. If they refuse to obey, they will be compelled to leave the island; and if they withdraw, they will let the Roman (Greek) people stray toward the precipices, without pastors and without leaders.[71]

History records that a number of clerics and laymen interrupted the proceedings of the patriarch and the synod, reminding them that they, too, had suffered at the hands of the Latins since the conquest of Constantinople and that an act of homage was not a mere gesture, but an admission of complete surrender and submission.[72] Further widening the breach between Latins and Greeks, in July of 1229, Patriarch Germanos of Constantinople sent a letter addressed this time to the Syrians and the Greeks.[73] The patriarch warned the Cypriots that by submitting to the Latins and following their innovations, they,too, became heretics because: 1) the Latin Church had broken away from the decisions of the Ecumenical Synods; 2) the Latin Church had invented new dogmas; and 3) the Latin Church had set up the pope in the place of Christ.[74]

In 1231 the Latins burned thirteen monks at the stake. Papaioannou gives a detailed account of this incident and points out that the narrative from which he takes the story is not a contemporary account.[75] John and Konon, two monks from Mount Athos, came to Cyprus to share the sufferings and misfortunes of their co-believers. The monks settled at Kantara Monastery, or Monastery of the Virgin Mary at Kantara. Soon other monks joined them. Andrew, a Dominican friar, also went to this monastery to debate the question whether the Church should use leavened or unleavened bread in the Eucharist.[76] The Orthodox maintained that only "enzyma" or leavened bread as they received it from their forefathers was scripturally correct and that all the Ecumenical Synods confirmed it. The use of unleavened bread, they said, had no scriptural authority, and the Latins, who followed the practice, were "heretical." At this point the Orthodox suggested that the issue be resolved by "trial by ordeal" or "trial by fire." One of the Greek monks and one of the Latins, preferably Andrew, would hold the Eucharist, according to his own rite and proceed to walk through a burning fire.[77] He who emerged unscathed would represent the true faith. Andrew refused to accept the challenge and ordered the monks to go to Nicosia and to appear before the Latin archbishop. When asked to explain their position, the monks maintained that whoever received "azyma" for Holy Communion was a heretic. The Latin archbishop ordered the authorities to throw them into prison hoping that the monks might change their minds. The Latins beat and tortured them during the three years of their incarceration. One of the monks, Theodoret from Athos, died. Eustorge left the island for a while and went to Acre to settle a dispute with Balian d'Ibelin whom the pope had excommunicated for having married Eschive de Montéliard within the third and fourth degrees of consanguinity.[78] Eustorge left Andrew to deal with the monks, and, having related their obstinacy to King Henry, received permission to do whatever he saw fit with them. Andrew professed that he could not rightfully inflict the death sentences. He instructed the authorities to tie the monks

to the tails of horses and mules and drag the monks through
the market place and the river. Finally, they were burned at
the stake. Leo Allatius, a Greek from the island of Chios, who
defected to the Latins and whom the Latins appointed librarian
of the Vatican in 1661 under Pope Alexander VII, rationalized
and justified the tragedy.[79]

On April 9, 1240, the king of Cyprus received a letter from
Pope Gregory IX demanding that no Greek cleric be allowed
to celebrate the Eucharist in his respective diocese until the
cleric renounced his heresies, especially concerning the use of
leavened bread in Communion.[80] The policy of the Holy See
changed with the elevation of Pope Innocent IV (1243-1254).
This change was the result of the friendly relations between
John Vatatzes, emperor at Nikaia, and Frederick II Hohen-
staufen, son of Henry VI. Since both were enemies of the
papacy and were hostile to the Latin empire of Constantinople, the papacy saw a means of union between the Eastern
and Western churches and cultures. Frederick was hostile
toward the Latin Empire because he saw in it one of the
elements of papal power and influence. Vatatzes considered
the pope an adversary who, by refusing to recognize the Orthodox patriarchate of Constantinople established at that time
at Nikaia, was creating a serious obstacle to Vatatzes' aim of
taking possession of Constantinople. Both, however, were pur-
suing different aims:[81] Frederick wished the papacy to renounce its claim to secular power; Vatatzes hoped that, by virtue of compromise, the West would recognize the Church. In
this way the Latin patriarchate at Constantinople would lose
its raison d' être. The Latin Empire hopefully would gradually disappear. This possibility obviously alarmed the papacy,
for in 1247 Innocent appointed the Franciscan brother
Lawrence, his penitentiary, as his official legate to the East,
including Cyprus, and ordered him to protect the Greeks from
any harm by the Latins.[82] In accordance with this, Greeks
who had left the island and wished to return and pay obedience
to Rome could do so under protection of the pope.[83]

The new legate, Eudes de Chateauroux, cardinal bishop of

Tusculum, who arrived in Cyprus with Louis IX (1226-1270) and his crusaders in 1248, furthered this conciliatory policy. Even the Greek archbishop with his clergy came and paid homage to the king and to the legate of the Latin Church. Apparently, this acknowledgement had its ulterior motive in the form of a series of demands which apparently were forwarded to the pope. Two years later Pope Innocent set forth what appear to be responses to the demands.[84]

1. The constitution of Pelagius was to be suppressed.

2. Tithes were to be restored to the Greeks.

3. The fourteen original dioceses were to be re-established according to the ancient canons before the arrival of the Latins. The Latin successors to the earlier archbishops of the island were to be stricken from the lists and only these earlier prelates were to be commemorated in the diptychs.[85]

4. Greek bishops were to recover their old jurisdictions. No restrictions were to be placed on a candidate's taking orders or becoming a monk.

5. Appeals from the decision of the Greek bishops were to go directly to the pope and not to the Latin bishops or the legate.

6. Amnesty was to be granted to those whom the Latins had punished for disobedience.

Temporarily the Greeks received encouragement from the conciliatory attitude of Eudes de Chateauroux and Louis IX, whom Innocent had asked to look into these demands. The new Latin archbishop, Hugh of Fagiano,[86] however, curtailed any further hopes the Greeks had of obtaining concessions. He ignored the order of Pope Innocent IV to win the Greeks through consultation and reconciliation, rather than coercion. On Palm Sunday, April 9, 1251, against the conciliatory policy of Innocent IV, Hugh gathered all the Cypriot Greeks in the Latin cathedral and, using the threat of excommunication, commanded all the Greeks whom the Latin Church had married and confirmed to attend the Latin mass in the Cathedral of Hagia Sophia every Sunday, to confess to a Latin priest at least once a year, and to receive the sacraments of the Church according to the Latin rite. This same threat applied to all Greek priests and deacons who refused obedience to the Latin Church.[87]

De Mas Latrie mentions that at this time the Greek archbishopric was vacant and that the pope had granted permission to the Greek bishops to elect a successor.[88] They elected Germanos Pesimandros,[89] who was consecrated by the suffragan Greek bishops in the name of the Latin Church. Pesimandros promised obedience to Rome. The bishops, in turn, would be answerable to Germanos with the implication that they would ignore the Latin archbishop of Nicosia.[90] Disgusted and unable to gain support against these concessions of the pope, Hugh placed the island under interdict and retired to his native Italy. From this time until his return after King Henry's death on January 18, 1253, numerous disputes arose between Latins and Greeks concerning sacraments, rites, and ceremonies which Cardinal Eudes mediated.[91] According to J. L. La Monte, King Henry died on January 18, 1253; and the executors of his estate were Guy d'Ibelin, Philip de Novaro and Robert de Montguiscard, according to his last will and testament.[92] Apparently, Henry had withheld the tithes of the churches of the diocese of Limassol and Nicosia. Pope Alexander IV (1254-1261) commissioned the bishop and archdeacon of Acre in a letter dated May 14, 1255, to be responsible that the executors:

> . . . carry out the dying wish of the late king to restore to the churches of Limassol and Nicosia the tithes belonging to them which the king had withheld during his lifetime. If the executors refuse to comply, let them be excommunicated.[93]

When Innocent IV died on December 7, 1254, his conciliatory policies died with him; when Alexander IV succeeded him, Hugh took up his persecution of Germanos and the Greeks with the apparent approval of the pope.[94] Hill defends the *Bulla Constitutio* of the pope as a document in favor of the

Greeks.[95] According to this document, the Latins should exact an oath of obedience to the Latin Church in a prescribed
form:

> I . . ., Bishop of . . ., from this time forward will be faithful
> and obedient to Blessed Peter and the Holy Roman Church,
> and to my Lord (name), archbishop of Nicosia, and to his
> successors canonically appointed. I will not be privy to any
> plot or act whereby they may lose life or limb or suffer any
> loss. Any purpose which the shall reveal to me, either per-
> sonally or by messenger or letter, I will not make known
> to anyone to their disadvantage. I will assist in defending
> and maintaining the supremacy of the Church of Rome and
> the primacy of the Church of Nicosia and the ordinances
> of the holy fathers against all men, my privileges being
> safeguarded. When summoned by the Synod, I will attend
> unless hindered by any canonical impediment. The legate
> of the Apostolic See, when he shall be duly notified to me,
> I will treat respectfully both when going and returning,
> and I will assist him in all his wants. So help me God and
> these holy Gospels.[96]

Still not satisfied with the provisions of the *Constitutio
Cypria,* Hugh of Fagiano resigned his post in 1263 and returned to Italy two years after the Greek troops of Michael
VIII Palaiologos (1261-1282) had captured and occupied Constantinople (July 25, 1261). Three weeks later, to the delight
of all Cypriots, as well as of the whole Byzantine world,
Michael, the "New Constantine" and second founder of Constantinople, as he called himself, entered the capital on August
15, 1261, the feast day of the Dormition of the Virgin Mary.
Michael now moved the empire from Nikaia to Constantinople. As a protection against the Venetians, Michael negotiated
a treaty with the Genoese, in accordance with the treaty of
Nymphaion.[97] Apparently aware that the fall of the Latin empire in Constantinople had given the Greeks a resurgence of
energy, now that the papacy suffered not only a loss of political

prestige, but also severe damage to its spiritual authority, Pope Urban IV (proclaimed pope on August 29, 1261) sought to curb any problems with the Greeks on Cyprus. On January 3, 1263, the pope sent a letter to the archbishop of Nicosia stating that he should exercise his jurisdiction in matters of ecclesiastical discipline over the laity, "notwithstanding the opposition of the secular authorities."[98] In this letter the pope charged the archbishop to extirpate heresy among the Greeks, as well as the Syrians. In response to the fact that the Cypriot Greeks were attacking and threatening their own clergy who were conforming to the Latin rulers, on January 23, 1263, the pope wrote to the bailli of Cyprus asking him to protect the Greeks who had accepted the Latin rite and to assist the archbishop of Nicosia.[99] According to a letter written by Urban to the bailli of Cyprus and dated April 13, 1264, the Latin archbishop of Nicosia went to Orvieto, the papal residence. During this visit the archbishop informed the pope of problems on Cyprus, which arose from the fact that the bailli had refused to help him in implementing the *Constitutio Cypria*.[100]

New circumstances now altered the relations between Emperor Michael Palaiologos and the Latin West. Following the famous battle of Benevento (February 26, 1266) in which Charles of Anjou defeated Manfred and became king of Sicily, Charles threatened the Eastern Empire and made no secret of the fact that he wished to bring the Greek East under his sovereignty. On May 24, 1267, a treaty was drawn up between William of Villehardouin and Charles; three days, later, another treaty, between Baldwin II and Charles was made. William of Villehardouin had met Charles of Anjou on an Egyptian crusade, and his first wife, the granddaughter of Agnes of France, was Charles' cousin. Baldwin II was the former Latin emperor of Constantinople. In both treaties, all the Greek lands still in the power of the Latins passed under the domination of Charles, the new king of Sicily.[101] The papacy and Venice also became part of a coalition. Consequently, from 1266 until his death in 1282, Michael devoted his complete attention to the defeat of Charles, whose ambitions would have brought the final destruction of the Byzantine Empire. This conflict threw in the balance the entire resources of not only each state but also the whole Mediterranean area, from Castile to Aragon in the West, to Egypt and Cyprus in the East. The key event affecting Michael's relations with the West was the signing of two treaties whose purpose was the restoration of the Latin empire of Romania. The first treaty intended to transfer the suzerainty of the principality of Morea in Greece to Charles.[102] The second treaty, signed by Baldwin II and Charles of Anjou, was a blueprint for the conquest of the Byzantine Empire,[103] bringing together Charles, Baldwin, William of Achaia, and the pope (all three threats to Michael and his empire). The provisions of this treaty would have made Charles master of the Byzantine Empire. He would have been able to use bases in the Aegean Sea, from which he could move by sea directly on Constantinople. To counteract this situation, Michael established a firm alliance with the Genoese at Galata (1267) and with the Venetians (Greco-Venetian Treaty of 1268).[104] In 1269 Charles signed a treaty with King Bela IV of Hungary, forcing Michael to turn for help to Charles' brother, Louis IX. Michael resorted to a church union in order to save his empire. Pope Gregory X and Michael Palaiologos initiated negotiations prompted by Michael's conviction that only such an accord could avert the menace of Charles of Anjou's threatened invasion of the empire. "It was clear that the Emperor sought the union only from fear of Charles; otherwise it would never have entered his mind."[105] According to accounts of contemporary historians, had the papacy permitted Charles of Anjou to launch a full-scale expedition, Constantinople, and with it Cyprus, would surely have fallen into his hands.[106] On July 6, 1274, Pope Gregory X and the representatives of Emperor Michael Palaiologos achieved the union of the Roman and Greek churches at the Council of Lyons. To this Council came, among others, "Archiepiscopus Nicosiensis"[107] who signed the minutes recognizing the Roman primacy. Michael suggested that the Greeks should have friendly relations with Rome. Only the Greek hierarchy, however, accepted this union with Rome.[108] The remainder of the Greek East from the clergy to the laity remained firm in their opposition to the union, believing that any kind of union would bring not only imposition of *filioque,* but also adoption of the Latin practices. Any conciliatory policy for Cypriot Greeks meant continued subjugation of the island to the Latin West. This policy apparently continued even after Lyons. On October 26, 1280, Matthew, archbishop of Caesarea, sent a letter ratifying the decree of 1253 by Hugh, archbishop of Nicosia, and Odo, bishop of Tusculum and apostolic legate. He made provisions to excommunicate any "disturbers of holy services." Matthew made attendance mandatory at the Latin church of Hagia Sophia, instead of at 'private chapels' and 'abbey churches.'[109] To dominate the Greek Cypriots further, in 1280 the Latin Archbishop Raphael issued a constitution giving instructions to the Greeks of the island for their discipline, church rituals, and administration, which the Greek bishops should read four times a year to clergy and laity.[110]

In 1291 the reign of the Latin states came to an end with the fall of Acre. John Furco of Ancona, the archbishop of Cyprus, complained of the interference of the Latin patriarch of Jerusalem whose representatives were in Nicosia collecting tithes. Pope Nicholas IV ordered that the Latins should return the monies collected to the archbishop of Nicosia,[111] whose existence depended on these revenues. Apparently, the attempt to sustain the archbishopric of Nicosia failed, for, as Hill points out,[112] archbishops were absent from Cyprus for thirty-six of the sixty-nine years between 1291 and 1360.

Cyprus, then, played a significant role in thirteenth-century crusading history from the establishment of the Latin Church in 1196 to the fall of the Latin states on the mainland. In its institutions the kingdom of Cyprus became an heir of the Latin patriarchate of Constantinople and the kingdom of Jerusalem. Latin rulers treated their Greek subjects at times with toleration and moderation and at other times resorted to persecution and coercion, depending on whether they were to be viewed as heretics or schismatics. The policy, therefore, was one of vacillation between forceful submission and cajoling diplomacy. From the point of view of the Cypriot clergy, heirs of the Byzantine tradition, a conflict between two divergent conceptions of the Church was the basis for the opposition between Latins and Greeks. To the monarchical claims of the Latin archbishops, heirs of the papal tradition, was opposed the Byzantine concept of pentarchy, according to which the patriarchs in the East, while acknowledging the honorary primacy of old Rome, rejected papal assertions of universal jurisdiction which would have constituted the bishops of the East as subservient arms of the Holy See. In the West the pope alone had supreme ecclesiastical jurisdiction according to the canonistic development of the papacy. In the East the first seven Ecumenical Synods which represented the infallible repository of ecclesiastical doctrine comprised the highest religious authority.[113] After 1204 the attitude of the populace, as seen in Constantinople, as well as on Cyprus, was one of devotion to the person of the emperor who was the living symbol of the continuity of the empire. An attack on the faith in any given place, such as on the remote island of Cyprus where faith, culture and language were Greek, was therefore an attack on the destiny and fortunes of the Empire itself. The Byzantines believed that much of the Empire was under special protection of the blessed Theotokos, Mother of God. Her mediation with her divine Son wrought miracles.[114] Cyprus had fallen to the Latins. Many Greeks believed that this event resulted from the sins of the Greek people, which made God angry. Understandably the Greeks must have reasoned that the Cypriot element of the empire would certainly crumble if they altered the purity of the faith through adoption of Latin confessions, such as the *Constitutio Cypria*. A more implicit explanation for the resistance to union was the popular sentiment that it was the prologue to the Latinization of the Greek Church and laity, which meant not only ecclesiastical apostasy but betrayal of the Greek sense of national pride.

Chapter Three

CYPRUS AND CONSTANTINOPLE

In northern France, the British Isles, and Sicily, the native population gradually assimilated the Norman aristocracy. A large portion of the leaders came from the citizens of these areas. The Frankish aristocracy of Cyprus followed a similar pattern. On Cyprus, however, religious differences played a key role. In Ireland, for example, Protestant English conquerors differed only slightly from the natives. English and Irish intermarried frequently. Cypriots resembled the Irish in their religious attitudes. The Church became a bulwark against cultural domination. The clergy was held in high esteem during this time, especially in political matters when the invaders either drove out the secular leaders of forced them to compromise. From the native Cypriot viewpoint, the Lusignan period was basically one of struggle between the Greek Orthodox and Latin Catholic churches. In 1196 the Pope Celestine III issued a papal bull in which he designated the organization and establishment of the Roman Catholic Church on Cyprus.[1] Three years later Alexios III drafted the 'Chrysobull of 1199' which was a premeditated plan to conquer the Greek East and divide the territory between the Venetians and the Latins.[2] The Latin conquest of Constantinople in 1204 brought to a natural climax the age-old political, ecclesiastical and commercial rivarly between Greek and Latin Christendom. After the ruthless sack of the capital, the Latins partitioned the empire into territories.[3] This division epitomized the conflict, latent at first and finally open, between Latin West and Byzantium and led to the ultimate destruction of the Byzantine Empire. The crusaders were not solely responsible for the catastrophe; many enemies from without weakened Byzantium. The new crusade in 1203 was originally intended to reconquer the Holy Land as well as to subjugate the Byzantine Greeks of Constantinople. The ambition and rancor of Venice actually deflected this Crusade.[4] Pope Innocent III protested ineffectively against the scandalous transformation of a holy war into an excuse for plunder. The crusader barons found themselves in an uncompromising position with the Venetians. Villehardouin's chronicle shows that the crusaders accepted all the Venetian propaganda and, despite the pope's remonstrances, succeeded in rationalizing away their evil intentions.[5] The contempt for Byzantium, which had been mounting during more than a century of wars in the East, appeared finally to have justified the launching of armies against a Christian country. The crusaders sacked the city, defiled sanctuaries, raped, and murdered citizens. Niketas Choniates, an eyewitness to the siege of Constantinople, gives a striking picture of the crusaders' pillaging and seizure of priests, monks, and abbots with the comment that even the Muslims had been more merciful in the seige and capture of Jerusalem than the Latins who claimed to be the soldiers of Christ.[6] Villehardouin commented: "Since the world was created, never had so much booty been won in any city."[7] The Fourth Crusade had come a long way from Ecry, where the Crusade had first been preached.[8] Its termination without confronting a single armed Muslim appalled poets and writers.[9]

As early as 1097, Alexios Komnenos had been afraid that the Latin barbarians would seize his capital. In 1146, Manuel Komnenos feared the Germans and the French more than he feared the Turks. He favored a reconciliation with the West and relied heavily on his alliances with the Franks as well as with Italian merchant republics. In 1176 his defeat at

Myriokephalon by the Turks of Kilij Arslan II struck a decisive blow at his policies and his prestige.[10] After Manuel's death in 1180, and the short regency of his widow, Maria of Antioch, Manuel's cousin Andronikos seized power and broke with the Latins. His reign began with popular uprisings, in the course of which almost the whole of the Italian colony at Constantinople (numbering thousands) was massacred.[11] Andronikos died tragically two years later in 1185. The aristocratic party of Constantinople overthrew him and had him lynched with unprecedented savagery by the populous despite the fact that in him the people lost one of the few emperors who would have defended them against the nobles.

With the elimination of the Komneni, the imperial throne was vulnerable to the intrigues of the nobles and occupied by individuals possessing neither authority nor prestige: Isaak Angelos and his son Alexios after him. Cyprus could no longer rely on the assistance of Constantinople, which was too occupied with internal struggles, the wars against the Normans, and the growing hostility of Venice. By 1204 Western feelings at the loss of the Holy Land had become blunted; the great crusading army was busy building a new Latin empire at Constantinople.

Admittedly the crusades were a major factor in the endeavor to trace the course of the slow deterioration in relations between Greeks and Latins on Cyprus and in the East in general. The crusades made apparent the old antagonism between the two Christian civilizations. The crusades of the thirteenth century did not entirely end in failure because Islam had become stronger and Christendom weaker, but in consequence of the ruin of Byzantium.

In the West after the planning of 1199 and the change of direction and the crusade in 1203, much of the former enthusiasm for the Holy Land had been lost. The idea had been a pious dream and not a necessity. Christianity did not sing songs of triumph when Frederick II obtained Jerusalem through a treaty which actually placed the city under the rule of a Christian monarch. Songs of triumph were reserved for the tiny kingdom of Cyprus. The kingdom under the Lusignans, short-lived though it was, stood for the positive side of the crusading movement, which by this time resorted to subjugating of Christian brethren to the papacy. The infiltration of foreigners in Cyprus and Constantinople provided the young nations of the West with a common ideal. This ideal, consciously or unconsciously was always the saving grace of the pope and the church and lay at the root of all foreign migration to the East. This surge of mystical feeling in politics, in which material aspirations were overlaid with a veneer of mysticism, cannot be considered unique in history. Cyprus affords one the opportunity to see that rarely have the two motives been so perfectly fused. Indirectly, but quite clearly, Latin and Frankish occupation of the East acted as a catalyst on the national pride of the Western peoples. United by religious adherence to the papacy in a common cause, these peoples learned to know one another better and also to hate one another. They learned even more to hate their great ally and rival, the empire of Byzantium.

Any deep sense of rational pride finds a need to seek something more than glory and prosperity for its native land and to go beyond the idea of the nation itself. In this light, the impulse to establish a Latin patriarchate in Constantinople and on Cyprus was one factor in the creation of Western rationalism which would interact with Greek national pride. As a result, because they differed from the inhabitants of Cyprus, Western Europeans produced a form of religion which differed in essential respects from the Eastern Orthodox and bore even less resemblance to the primitive church. The feudal society of the West had to accomodate a vigorous class of nobles, whose collective power balanced that of their monarchs. However, the power of the Byzantine emperor was limited only by inefficiency or the necessity to compromise. In effect, the war-bands of pagan Europe still existed, though their energies were chanelled in organizational patterns influenced by the example of the Roman world.[12] Moreover, in the West, particularly in the Italian city-states, an uneasy balance existed between secular and clerical power. This balance made possible the development of specifically secular modes of thought. The Rennaisance and scientific revolution in the West did not occur by accident.

The Greeks benefited to some extent from the balance of power between the Lusignan state and the Latin Church, which adopted the feudal practices of the West. Following the election of Baldwin of Flanders and Hainaut as Latin emperor of Constantinople in 1204, Cyprus adopted feudal and criminal codes introduced into the East by Baldwin from his native Hainaut. The fourteen administrative divisions of the island under the Byzantines were reduced to twelve after the beginning of the Frankish period.[13] These twelve districts were grouped into four provinces, administered in the time of Hugh IV by four baillies. Afterwards each district had its own magistrate.[14] According to the Bull of 1196, Nicosia the capitial, also became the seat of the Latin Church and the archbishop. The codes helped in the balance of power to keep as much peace on the island as possible. In fact, in spite of papal prohibition, the king laid taxes upon the Latin clergy from time to time. Cyprus adopted Baldwin's principle of reducing the Church's interference with their Orthodox subjects on whom they depended for rent money and other feudal dues. In 1223 Philip d' Ibelin, as co-regent, objected to the Latin oppression of Greeks. In 1264 the regent, Hugh of Antioch, citing the Baldwinian criminal codes, excused himself from helping the Latin archbishop to inflict punishment on the Greeks, insisting that the permission of the *Haute Cour* was necessary in such a case.[15] The Lusignan period, beginning with Guy in 1192, lost much of its vigor after the assassination of Peter I in 1369. Because society was organized on a hierarchical basis like the pattern of Constantinople, relative stability was maintained, despite the rivalry of the Frankish nobles. One must study the system of Baldwin to see how the prosperity of the island depended on the ability of the Franks to hold the island by force since no tribute was sent abroad for the first time in twelve hundred years. The feudal system of the Latin patriarchate

and of Constantinople is most prefectly exemplified in the
kingdom of Cyprus, which retained the system of the Venetian period, long after it had crumbled elsewhere. Government
was in the hands of a *Haute Cour,* comprising the entire body
of barons, who possessed executive, legal and judicial powers.
The king or his representative presided. Most of the barons,
like Guy himself, were Franks who had been forced out of
Palestine or Syria.[16]

Since Baldwin played such an important role in the new
Latin Empire, a brief history of his life is necessary. Born in
1172, he was the son of Baldwin V, count of Hainaut, who in
1169 had married Margaret, sister of Philip of Alsace, count
of Flanders.[17] Baldwin's reign in Flanders and Hainaut lasted
only seven years, until April 14, 1202, when he left for the
crusade. Villehardouin related that the most significant
developments of his reign took place before Ash Wednesday,
February 23, 1200, the year he "took the cross."[18] Robert L.
Wolff made a most interesting study of Baldwin's life in which
he cites new sources. In these sources he has uncovered two
important charters for Hainaut, which historians regard as the
foundation of both the feudal and the criminal law of that
region. The charters are among the earliest attempts to codify
what had been, until then, a mere conglomeration of ancient
unwritten custom.[19] Baldwin issued these charters as an attempt to simplify the task of administering Hainaut while the
count was away on the crusade. Their importance lies in the
fact that few documents survive telling of feudal codes design-
ed to prevent the outbreak of private war while the lords and
counts were away on a crusade. The charters provided a clear
set of rules governing the inheritance of fiefs. The criminal
code reduced the temptation for the always turbulent magnates
of the county to disturb the peace by providing a clear set of
penalties for murder and mutilation.[20] The charter begins:
"Hoc est forma pacis in toto Comitatu Hainoense" and is a
summary of criminal law. According to this "forma pacis,"[21]
people who are not knights or sons of knights pay a life for
a life and a limb for a limb. The lord or the relatives of a man

killed defending himself against an attacker shall exact no revenge. If a homicide flees, his relatives and friends must formally abandon and forswear him; the authorities regard anyone who fails to do so in the same category as the wanted criminal until he shall so renounce the culprit. In the case of the loss of limb, the procedure was the same: friends and family of the criminal must forswear him; those of the victim must offer assurances to those who have so forsworn the criminal. Other pertinent factors exist in his second chapter (e.g., pertaining to lords, to murders, to the carrying of pointed weapons, etc.)

The importance of these two charters lies not so much in their effect on the lands of Hainaut in the absence of Baldwin, but in the surviving legislation during the partitioning of the empire by the "Partitio Romaniae." According to the "Partitio," the new emperor received one quarter of the empire, while the Venetians and the non-Venetian crusaders divided the remaining three quarters. Although the doge himself would take no oath to do so the vassals would also determine, the distribution of fiefs. In all these territories the emperor was ultimately responsible for justice; the system of the "baillis," as found in the charters of Hainaut, was the basis for the legislative system. In this context historians remember Baldwin most of all as a lawgiver in his short reign as emperor.[22]

In 1186 Baldwin married Marie, daughter of Count Henri of Champagne and sister of Thibaut, predecessor of Boniface of Montferrat as commander-in-chief of the armies of the Fourth Crusade. She was twelve years old at the time of their wedding and had been betrothed to Baldwin almost since birth. Contemporary chroniclers all attest to the fact that the marriage was very happy, apparently, despite the age difference.[23] Villehardouin gives some information concerning Marie. She, too, had taken up the cross about the same time as Baldwin.[24] Because she was pregnant, she was unable to leave Flanders until early 1204, leaving behind two daughters, Jeanne, born in 1199, and Margaret, born in 1202. Unaware that the crusaders had been diverted to Byzantium instead of going to Palestine, Marie sailed from Marseilles and arrived at

Acre in the summer of 1204, only to hear that Baldwin was
now Latin emperor of Constantinople. At Acre Marie apparently settled the conflict between King Leo of Cilician Armenia
and Prince Bohemond V of Antioch. She undertook this respon-
sibility because Antioch had been a fief of the Byzantine Empire and now belonged to Baldwin as successor to the Byzantine emperors.[25] In August of 1204, she died of the plague,
which had broken out in Acre, and Baldwin returned her body
to Constantinople.

In April 1205, Ioannitsa, king of the Vlachs and the
Bulgarians, captured Baldwin near Adrianople. Villehardouin
and Niketas Choniates are in complete agreement about this
episode. Robert of Clari says that Baldwin was lost and his
fate unknown.[27] Ernoul, not the most reliable chronicler in
the opinion of most historians, says that Ioannitsa killed
Baldwin in battle.[28] Villehardouin, nevertheless, relates that,
convinced of Baldwin's death, the barons, with the consent
of the Venetians, crowned Baldwin's brother, Henry, as the
new emperor on August 10, 1206, in the Cathedral of Hagia
Sophia.[29]

With this brief history of Baldwin, the first elected emperor
of the Latin Empire, if one would follow the legislative procedures in each of the divided territories according to the "Partitio Romaniae,"[30] one could see the influence which Flanders
and Hainaut had in the matter. The *Book of the Customs of
the Empire of Romania* — a codification of the Assizes made
apparently in the first quarter of the fourteenth century under
the auspices of the Angevins and still surviving in a Venetian
version a century later[31] — reveals the workings of the feudal
system in the principality of Achaia. Here the chief source is
that collection of documents called the *Chronicle of Morea.*
These documents, derived probably from one common original,
are unique for the appreciation of the whole period in the relations of the Latins and the Greeks following the conquest of
the Morea. In the prologue is a description of the preliminary
history of the crusade which terminated in the Latin conquest
of Constantinople. The *Chronicle* is most informative about

the Frankish court and judicial systems. Glarenza then consisted of a flourishing market place with its own weights and measures and was the residence of Italian bankers known throughout the Mediterranean. In a similar manner, the palace of Mistra was a flourishing palace of nobles, second only to Constantinople. The *Chronicle* describes the great castles of Chloumoutsi and Passava, Kantara and Kyrenia on Cyprus and the lives and wars of the Western nobles. The *Chronicle* also reveals how Latin monks in the monasteries of Isova, Bella Paese or St. Hilarion fared in these lands of their adoption. The *Chronicle* constitutes one more witness, however, to the fact that the Frankish conquest left few points of contact with the people of Greece with whom they never really amalgamated. They differed in origin, creed, customs, and language; and Latin policy of many Western rulers did not succeed in bridging the chasm between East and West.

In this system the following compromised society: the prince, the holders of the twelve great baronies ("bers de terre") the greater and lesser vassals ("ligili" and "himnes plani homgii'), among whom were the conquered Byzantines (freedmen and serfs). The legal systems were similar to those in Hainaut and Flanders, as well as to those embodied in the "Assizes of Jerusalem" a century earlier.[32] The *Chronicle of Morea* indicates that in the conquest the Franks borrowed the system of the 'assizes' which Aimery de Lusignan used on Cyprus.[33]

The Partition Treaty of March 1204 had set down the procedure for the election of the Latin emperor and had alloted him, besides the Byzantine imperial palaces in the capital, only one quarter of the empire. At the very outset, the Latin Empire had problems. The Venetian and non-Venetian crusaders would divide the remaining three quarters. The doge himself would take no oath to render service to the emperor, nor would the emperor participate in the distribution of fiefs. A mixed committee of crusaders and Venetians would distribute them.

The Partition Treaty divided the spoils with the lion's share going to Venice. According to the treaty, the Venetian clergy received the Church of Hagia Sophia, and a Venetian, Thomas Morosini, became the patriarch, head of the Roman Church in the new Empire.

The results of the partitioning of the Empire had far-reaching effects. The Franks formed the Latin empire of Constantinople, the kingdom of Thessalonike, the principality of Achaia in the Peloponnesos (Morea), and the duchy of Athens and Thebes in central Greece. Venice's rule extended inland as well as to the Aegean and Ionian islands. Along with the Latin feudal possessions on former Byzantine lands, the Byzantines formed three independent centers: the empire of Nikaia, the empire of Trebizond (both in Asia Minor), and the despotate of Epiros in northern Greece.

The capture of Constantinople by the crusaders and the establishment of the Latin Empire put the pope in a difficult position. Innocent III had opposed the forceful taking and destruction of Constantinople and had even excommunicated the crusaders and Venetians as early as the Zara episode. After the fall of the capital city, however, he stood face to face with a *fait accompli*. His main concern now was to win over the Greeks by persuasion and gentle treatment. The excesses of the Latins in the sack of Constantinople naturally distressed him.[34] This initial empathy with the conquered Greeks is especially important because it involves much more than that found in the superficial treatment given to the subject by many historians.

On August 2, 1206, Pope Innocent III wrote to the first Latin patriarch, Thomas Morosini, suggesting that he win over the recalcitrant bishops of "Romania" through diplomacy. Only if this procedure proved unsuccessful should he and the Cardinal legate, Benedict of Santa Susanna, proceed to excommunicate and remove the Greek bishops from their sees and replace them with Latin appointees.[35] Obviously, the whole Christian East was reacting to Morosini whose actions appeared not only as papal policy, but also as a theological justification of aggression. The Easterners could still interpret the election of a Latin emperor in Byzantium as conforming with the laws of "war," but by virtue of an understood "right" or "custom" in the West, the pope appointed his own candidate to the see of St. John Chrysostom, New Rome.[36]

In a very short period of time, the East became aware of the ecclesiological development which had taken place in the West and which widened the apparent breach between the Latins and Byzantines.

Several documents, all directly connected with the appointment of the Venetian, Thomas Morosini, reveal the shock felt by the Byzantines:[37] (1) a letter to Innocent III by the deposed Byzantine patriarch of Constantinople, John Kamateros (1198-1206), who took refuge at Nikaia after the fall of the capital city; (2) a treatise, wrongly attributed to Photios (ninth century) and entitled, "Against those who Say that Rome is the First See"[38] (3) two writings of the learned Deacon Nicholas Mesarites, very similar in their contents to the pseudo-Photian treatise: the first, in the form of a dialogue with Morosini (which took place in Constantinople on August 30, 1206); the second, a pamphlet written when Nicholas was already the archbishop of Ephesos;[39] (4) the letter of a patriarch of Constantinople, whose name is unknown, to his colleague in Jerusalem;[40] (5) an article by an unknown Greek author: "Why Has the Latin Overcome Us?" This document attacks Morosini, giving many of the reasons why the Greeks particularly disliked him.

The writings are of interest because they reflect reactions of Greek theologians and choniclers to the actions of papal representatives, using the argument, for the most part, that St. Andrew founded Constantinople; therefore, his apostolicity ranks equally with Peter, who supposedly founded the see of Rome.[41] One may easily comprehend these writings and others when considering that the pope found it easier to suppress a bishopric than to revive one (even though there were exceptions to the rule, e.g., Theodore of Negropont). Even W. Miller emphasizes this conclusion throughout his book on the Latins in the Levant.[42] Examination of all available papal correspondence, as well as of secondary works in French,

English, and Greek, indicate that the Latins did not hesitate to reduce the number of Greek bishoprics by consolidating non-self-sustaining dioceses and diminishing the financial burden of the foreign conquerors. The Latin hierarchical organization in the patriarchate as a whole became very complicated. R. L. Wolff has performed a great service by compiling a list of tables which made the administration more understandable.[43] From a study of these tables, one can conclude that the Latins had greatly altered the previous hierarchical organization in every possible way. Wolff's study shows the most important change: the reduction in number of bishoprics and the unification of two sees. The Latins made numerous changes in the number and status of suffragan bishoprics under individual metropolitans. The Latins sometimes reduced Greek metropolitans as well as Greek autocephalous archbishoprics to the level of suffragan bishoprics only. They sometimes put suffragan sees under the jurisdiction of former Greek autocephalous archbishoprics which previously did not have them.[44]

These alterations in the Byzantine patriarchate of Constantinople also occurred in the "Partitio Romaniae" of 1204 and in the Chrysobull of 1198. The Latins had not yet established a patriarchate. The Chrysobull under section five and section six, a document attempting to serve the best interests of Venice, illustrates the breakdown.

Wolff has also created a list of four bishoprics,[45] contrasting four surviving letters of Innocent III, who confirms as bishoprics these formerly Greek metropolitan districts. The list of tables shows that the Latin bishoprics are far closer in number and identity to the Greek organization than is the "Provinciale Romanum."[46] Innocent lists the hierarchy as it should have been; the "Provinciale" as it was. The "Provinciale" further enhances the notion that Latin West and Byzantine Greek East were, in theory, an organic unit; as such, the Latins did not abandon the Greek hierarchical organization as an examination of the island of Cyprus shows, but rather utilized the structure to further the papacy's objectives.

In this light the capture of Constantinople by the crusaders and the establishment of the Latin Empire are premeditated events.[47] Innocent had revealed his views about the diversion of the crusade. After the fall of the capital of the Byzantine Empire, he was confronted by a *fait accompli*.[48] When the Latins conquered Constantinople, Baldwin notified the pope of the event with these words: "by the grace of God the Emperor of Constantinople and always Augustus," as well as "the Knight of the Pope."[49] The pope then called upon all clergy, all sovereigns and all peoples to support the cause of Baldwin and expressed the hope that, since the Latins had taken Constantinople, Westerners could more easily reconquer the Holy Land from the hands of the infidel. At the close of the letter the pope admonished Baldwin to be a faithful and obedient son of the Catholic Church.[50] Yet, when the pope learned in detail of the sack of Constantinople and when he realized that the "Partitio Romaniae" was a document basically secular in character with the intention of reducing the interference of the Church in all matters, Innocent wrote to the marquess of Montferrat:

> You have no right nor any jurisdiction over the Greeks and you seem to have unwisely deviated from the purity of your vow when you marched not against Saracens, but against Christians, with the intent not of conquering Jerusalem, but of taking Constantinople, preferring earthly riches to heavenly ones. More important is the fact that some [crusaders] spared neither religion, nor age, nor sex. . .[51]

Innocent realized, only too late, that the Latin Empire in the East, established on feudal grounds, possessed no strong political power, inasmuch as it had not thoroughly attained the prestige and economic objectives of the Western crusaders and merchants. Shortly after the partitioning of the empire, three independent Byzantine states emerged. The empire of Nikaia, under the dynasty of the Laskarids in the western part of Asia Minor, was situated between the Latin possessions in Asia

Minor and territories of the sultanate of Ikonion or Rum and possessed a part of the seashore of the Aegean. The Nikaian Empire was the largest of the Greek centers not under Western control and the most dangerous of the rivals of the Latin Empire.[52]

In 1204, on the southeastern shore of the Black Sea, David and Alexios Komnenos, who were grandsons of Emperor Andronikos I (1182-1185), founded the empire of Trebizond.

The one trend running through all of these established empires in the East was the feudal system, based on Western charters and traditions, and as introduced into the East by Baldwin of Flanders, the first Latin emperor of Constantinople. When new ideas of monarchy tending to absolutism prevailed in Europe, the barons on Cyprus re-established the old feudal custom.[53] All holders of fiefs were technically liegemen to the king, who could not punish a liege except by judgment of the *Haute Cour*. In comparing the systems of the Latin empire of Constantinople and those of the West, one sees that the system of parliaments never developed on Cyprus. All the holders of fiefs became peers, diminishing the power of tenants-in-chief. In matters of religion, marriage, and testaments, the nobles came before church courts. All cases involving non-noble Franks, including those which also involved noblemen, came before the *Cour des Bourgeois*, or *Basse Cour*.[54]

From the time of Guy de Lusignan, the fiefs and lands granted by the king to knights and nobles were of different values, according to the rank of the recipients. Many of those coming to Cyprus were knights who had been deprived of their fiefs by the Saracen conquests in Palestine and Syria. Widows and children of those nobles who died in the wars took advantage of Guy de Lusignan's open invitation that he would grant fiefs and lands to all who were willing to come and settle on the island.[55] On Cyprus a knight acquired a fief worth four hundred besants; an esquire, one worth three hundred; the same value was attached to the lands granted to the *sergents à cheval* and to the Turcopoles who owned two mounts and other accessories.[56] Guy de Lusignan, much to the dismay of Constantinople, which sought to regain Greek dominion over Cyprus, disposed of three hundred fiefs to knights and two hundred to *sergents à cheval*. He also made other grants to the common people who, as a result, flocked to the island.[57] In addition, Guy gave dowries to widows and orphan girls.[58]

This procedure on Cyprus created a situation which favored the Western domination and Latin rule on the island, and the feudal policies of Cyprus set the example for other kingdoms to follow. The Latin empire of Constantinople suffered because it did not follow through on the policies as set down by Baldwin, count of Flanders. Guy de Lusignan granted so many fiefs that only between twenty and seventy knights were left for the king to support.[59]

A new social order, established by the Franks and based on the Latin empire of Constantinople, resulted. No details of the lands which furnished the fiefs exist. Cypriots ceded to Richard I half of their possessions, which, naturally, were passed on to Guy, who also inherited the possessions of those natives who fled the island. The terms of the Council of Lemesos in 1220 clearly indicate that the crown and the barons held lands which belonged to Greek churches and monasteries prior to the French occupation.[60] By this time, little or no resistance to foreign suppresion by the Greeks occurred on Cyprus. No resistance arose because the spirit of the Greeks was completely crushed by their experiences in two attempts at revolt against Richard I and the Templars.[61]

3. Monastery of Apostle Andrew — 11th century

4. Kyrenia

5. Monastery of St. John Chrysostomos — 11th century

Chapter Four

CYPRUS AND LATIN THEOCRACY

The question that underlies the problem between Latin West and Greek East throughout this entire study is one of interpretation. The very fact that pronouncements by the pontiffs in the thirteenth century gave rise to such acute antagonism raises two possibilities for consideration. The first is that East and West simply fell into self-contradictions regarding ecclesiastical political theory. In that case, the very nature of the source material will probably ensure that conflicting interpretations of their ideas continue to plague scholars. The other possibility is that modern historians have not yet penetrated deeply enough into the texture of thirteenth-century thought, possibly out of fear of opening old wounds or even of inflicting new ones. This study concerns this second possibility, since science progresses on a philosophical plane not only by the accumulation of new evidence, but also by the acquisition of fresh insights, which grasp the relevance of evidence from a new point of view.

Scholars who return to the battlefield have not wasted their time belaboring a dead issue but have made the question itself a living and growing idea. Their work has been enhancing, and continued discussion and meditation on the aftermath of the Fourth Crusade in terms of West-East relations promise to be valuable and even thrilling. Most recently a few scholars have attempted to understand the motives behind these relations. They have taken into consideration the words and phrases, whose meaning remains the same for century after century, and have interpreted the concepts that they signified. These scholars have thus attempted to disregard the political, diplomatic, and economic preoccupations of earlier historians and have highlighted the friction between the emotions of the people and the calculations of responsible leaders in the thirteenth century. The leading exponent of "interior history," the effort to see events through the eyes of participants, is Paul Alphandery.[1]

The island of Cyprus becomes a prime example for modern scholarship on the Fourth Crusade. An analysis of the psychology of the crusading movement together with the sociological aspects, the hagiography, and the eschatology helps one see the currents of thought and emotion behind the Latin fervor to dominate. This work attempts to view Constantinople and Cyprus in this new dimension: the subjugation of one group of peoples by another in the name of unity, in which the great mystery concerning the Christian universe and its salvation is solved. The facts presented seem to emphasize one important point: the crusades and the Latin states in the East sought the ultimate unity, the destruction of evil and the reign of God. Before they could realize this unity, however, the East had to be conquered and forced to submit to the papacy. The Greeks, it was felt, stood in the way of this unity. The relationship between the Church and the Imperium was not, therefore, fortuitous, but essential.

The mediaeval thirteenth-century mind must be studied on its own terms, not only from an economic or political point of view, which the modern, secular-minded student of history seems to comprehend best, but from an analysis of the psychology of Latin overtures to the Greek East.[2] To view the diversion question, for example, only in terms of treason theories, as a triumph of human selfish passions, imposes modern stereotypes upon the past. If it is true that the problems of Church and State are still prevalent today, then

mediaeval concepts are in constant danger of distortion by
defining them in language that is overladen with specifically
modern connotations. If one analyzes the theories concerning
the Latin conquest of the East,[3] he will see that the difficulty lies in the employment of inadequate modern terminology
to characterize mediaeval ideas. In commonplace discussion
current words, such as "state," "dualism," "theocracy," or
"sovereignty," in addition to Latin and Greek phraseology,
can present problems difficult to overcome. Another difficulty is one of thought rather than language — the anachronistic
attempt to force mediaeval thought into the mold of modern
concepts of sovereignty. In the study of Constantinople and
Cyprus, the historian will readily note that the attempt to view
papal pronouncements as static formulations of law, which
would certainly make them more intelligible, would be misleading. Rather, one should view them as dynamic attempts
to bring about change in the existing Greek system and even-
tual unity with the "mystical" body of Christ. A view of Cyprus,
in particular, demonstrates that in modern interpretation of
thirteenth-century papal thought, consent was the objective.
The intent was to bring about effective change in the existing
structure of laws and rights. By approaching the political and
ecclesiastical thought of the thirteenth-century popes with
these considerations, one can see that their decretals were consistent with the mediaeval ideal of a universal papal monarchy, removed, however, from any modern theories of
sovereignty. In their pontificates, the popes issued pronouncements that seem, at first glance, to be uninhibited assertions of an extreme theocratic doctrine. From the time of
Gregory VII the popes repeatedly described themselves as
rulers set between God and men. Innocent III's intention in
the East was to base the church of the Vlacho-Bulgarian Empire, as well as that of the Latin Empire, on the Roman model.
His plan was obviously an extension of the Gelasian thought
that the priesthood was as superior to kingship as the soul is
to the body.

On Christmas Day, 1200, four centuries after the coronation

of Charlemagne, Innocent III summoned his cardinals to a secret consistory and read them a *Deliberatio* asserting that the empire pertained to the Roman See "first and last, principally and finally" — "principally" because the empire had been transferred to the West from Constantinople by the papacy, and "finally" because the emperor was "annointed," crowned, and invested with the empire by the pope.[4]

While theocratic principles seen from their decretals guided the popes in the ecclesiastical and secular politics of this age throughout their pontificates, at no time did the popes ever assert simply and lucidly that they were acting by virtue of a supreme temporal authority that was inherent in the pontifical office. In the correspondence or decretals cited and investigated in this study, when the pope mediated in a feudal dispute in Constantinople or on Cyprus, the reason given was always a question of impropriety, a breach of solemn oath, or a threat to the peace of Christendom. All of these matters were asserted to be the proper concern of the pope as head of the Church. Yet, at the same time, the papal intent was a conciliatory one: to avoid judgemental decrees which belonged to the local rulers and to avoid the tendency to usurp the rights of secular rulers because the powers of kings came from God. The contrast between these two positions became the story of thirteenth-century policy.

The problem of historians has constantly been one of reconciling these two positions. Even if one one succeeds in avoiding the problems of language, he leaves many problems of thought to unravel. If the pope had inherited the fullness of the power of Jesus Christ, who had been both priest and king, as Innocent III often liked to maintain, how could any assertion of political authority on his part constitute a usurpation? If, in the Byzantine sense, the emperor of Constantinople is the representative of God over God's kingdom on earth and is responsible for the Church as a kind of mediator between God and man on earth (as Eusebios envisaged it — "a vice-regent" of God),[5] how could any assertion of religious authority on his part constitute a usurpation? The prevalent point of view in works cited show popes such as Innocent III, Honorius III, Gregory IX, Celestine IV, Innocent IV, Alexander IV, and Urban IV as ambitious pretenders to a universal temporal lordship. Walter Ullmann has given this interpretation sophisticated formulation. He finds in the pontificate of Innocent III, for example, a re-affirmation of an older monistic tradition of the papacy at a time when some leading canonists were beginning to defend the autonomy of the secular power.[6] According to the argument, the popes were merely faithful followers of the theocratic doctrines expounded by great predecessors. This study has certainly confirmed this assertion, especially concerning the years following the First Crusade.

The popes acknowledged that the governance of human affairs required two orders of jurisdiction — a secular one and a spiritual one — and that normally each order ought to judge according to its own laws through its own courts in the cases appropriated to its own jurisdiction. Cyprus, with its internal evolution spilling over into new elements of continuity, showed that the problems posed by churchmen and crusaders in the thirteenth century also led to a disputed question encountered many times over in this work. Even if the popes acknowledged the need for two orders of jurisdiction, how did they conceive of the relationship between those two orders? Above all, did they regard the secular order as so subordinated to the spiritual that the head of the ecclesiastical hierarchy could, as was the case with the *Haute Cour,* take control of any kind of case and so determine the whole range of human activity?

On the other hand, this work has used the word "theocratic" repeatedly. Presumably a simple, unqualified "theocratic" doctrine would have asserted that the pope, as God's vicar on earth, possessed an absolute and unlimited authority over all men and all their affairs. Consequently, all legitimate authority was derived from the pope; and he could appoint and depose secular kings or their subordinate governors at will, hear appeals from their courts, enact secular legislation, settle disputes between temporal barons as a superior lord set over them or even abolish the structure of secular offices altogether and govern the world through clerical delegates. Interestingly enough, popes claimed some of these rights but not others. Since it was illicit for priests to shed blood, the popes always had to recognize the need for a permanently enduring order of temporal rulers who could actually exercise the "power of the sword." Yet, mediaeval pontiffs did, on occasion, claim the right to depose temporal rulers and to exercise secular jurisdiction. The historian's problem, therefore, is the one stated before: the emphasis is less and less on the popes' actual claims and more and more on the labels — "dualistic," "theocratic,""Caesaropapism," etc. — which should be attached to them.

John A. Watt indulges in this kind of argumentation to a great degree. He concedes that Innocent IV claimed a supreme appellate jurisdiction in temporal affairs. He then adds that the pope claimed this authority as a spiritual privilege divinely conferred on the Apostolic See; but he concludes his argument with an almost improbable twist. Since all of Innocent's claims were spiritual, Watt alleges that Innocent IV was a dualist after all.[7] Yet, Cyprus exemplifies that exactly the same argument can be used to prove the opposite. Innocent regarded his spiritual authority as all-encompassing and including jurisdiction over temporal cases of the *Haute Cour* since the king, in the name of the pope, accused Aimery Barlais, Amaury de Bethsan, Hugh de Giblet, Philip Chenart, and a number of others, of treason. The court declared them disinherited of their properties on Cyprus. Their fiefs were granted to supporters of the king and the papacy.[8] The cases in which royal jurisdiction was normally exercised corresponded to the exercise of the temporal jurisdiction of the papacy. In other words, any temporal intervention of the papacy outside of central Italy could very well have been regarded as an "indirect"consequence of its spiritual authority.[9]

This authority was not unusual because pontiffs of the thirteenth century believed firmly that powers originally conferred on the papacy by divine grant were not limited to the spiritual sphere but rather involved temporal jurisdiction.

If one bears in mind that a major task for the thirteenth-century popes was to maximize consent to a temporal jurisdiction, especially in lands far away from the Holy See, then the reasoning in the letters written to the princes and barons was obvious. When the popes sought to intervene in the disputes on Cyprus with the precedent established in the Latin patriarchate of Constantinople, as well as in the Latin kingdoms, they never relied on claims to general overlordship because they knew that any such pretention would have been angrily rejected by lay rulers. Rather, and particularly on Cyprus, they always found some "exceptional" reason, which the barons or lords themselves might be persuaded to accept, in order to justify their actions. Cardinal legate Pelagius, Queen Alice, Constable Walter of Caesarea and the barons of Cyprus would have indignantly denied that the pope was temporal overlord at the convention of Lemesos in 1220; but his claims to ecclesiastical policy governing, in essence, the goings-on on the whole island, and giving supremacy to the Latin Church were heeded. In this manner the property formerly belonging to the Greek clergy was possessed by the Latin clergy, and the nobles were to respect the rights of the Latin Church in these possessions. The civil power in Cyprus saw the difficulty of the situation and appealed to the pope to allow the Greek bishops to have authority over the Greeks.[10] To this request Pope Honorius replied that some of the Greeks had actually invaded Latin churches. In spite of the invasions, he would forgive and forget the actions of all those Greeks who had returned to the Roman Church. The popes also wrote to the patriarch of Jerusalem and to the archbishops of Tyre and Caesarea to provide that any recalcitant Greek bishops should be treated harshly in accordance with the agreement between the queen of Cyprus and the prelates of her kingdom.[11] Later, this request led to the break between the queen and her co-regent, Philip d'Ibelin. In this way, Cyprus found herself becoming a decentralized feudal kingdom which grew into an oligarchy of foreigners who took advantage of the extension of royal jurisdiction by the pope and of new procedures that kings and barons made available. The ease with which bishops, councils, and others could appeal to Rome stimulated the process of judicial supremacy over an unwilling Orthodox Church. The complexity of statements between the papacy and its representatives on Cyprus merely reflected the complexity of the task set out at the beginning of the Fourth Crusade. Brian Tierney observed that mediaeval popes, as theologians, could employ every resource of scriptural allegory and symbolism to proclaim all the height, breadth, and depth of papal power.[12] As politicians and diplomats, they had to work within the framework of public law that existed in their own day. As legislators, they could bring about effective changes in that law only by winning general consent for their proposals. Yet long before the Turkish conquest of Cyprus, the elder Sanudo observed that, though the Western powers might destroy the Byzantine Empire, they could not hold their conquests; the examples of Cyprus, Crete, the principality of Achaia, and the duchy of Athens showed that only the foreign conquerors, and not the native Greeks, belonged to the Roman faith.[13] The *Constitutio Cypria* attempted to settle the relationship of the two churches for the future, but it did not eliminate all the seeds of controversy. It reduced the Orthodox sees to four and provided that after the death of Patriarch Germanos, who was independent of the Latin hierarchy on the island, the Latin archbishop should be the sole metropolitan.[14]

The *Constitutio Cypria* brought no peace. Schism between the Orthodox and Latins endured. Orthodox who conformed were excommunicated by the Orthodox who resisted. The civil authorities refused to intervene to punish recusant Orthodox. The fear that, with the fall of Latin Constantinople, the new Byzantine emperor might take advantage of Cypriot disaffection to make a landing on Cyprus proved unfounded; but discontent smouldered, though no accute outbreak occurred until early in the next century.

The struggle continued and ended only when the Turks

expelled the Latins in the sixteenth century. The will of the indigenous Cypriots to survive as a distinct cultural entity was demonstrated by adherance to the one organized body left, namely the Orthodox Church. Concern for the interests of their own ethnic and religious group and hatred for apostasy which was equated with treachery towards the group kept many inside the native church. Those who remained might otherwise have been tempted by the advantages of joining the sect of their overlords.

6. Othello's Tower, built by the Lusignans

7. St. Hilarion Castle, summer residence of the Lusignans

8. Monastery of Stavrovouni — 4th century

Chapter Five

ORTHODOX AND LATINS:
ECCLESIASTICAL DIFFERENCES

The Latin-Greek schism before, during, and after the Fourth Crusade was a true schism in every sense of the word by the end of the thriteenth century. A mutual feeling of "brotherhood" existed; yet underlying this feeling was a sense of hostility and separation on the part of both sides. As Karmires, Congar, Every, and Runciman, among others, have noted, the fact of separation began almost from the foundation of Constantinople in 330. Constantine the Great never envisaged the city as a rival of Rome, which it became. Following the reign of Justinian (527-67), Constantinople and the church of the East assumed a distinct, non-Latin, Hellenic Christian role which historians term Byzantine. The West fell back on its continuing tradition of developing the hegemony of the Roman papacy which aided the development of Western culture known as mediaeval. As these cultures and their churches developed, they created antithetical institutions and roles. Finally, in the eleventh century the centralized authority of the papacy and the militant patriarchate of Constantinople clashed. While the incident of 1054 was not the cause of a Latin-Greek schism, it proved to be a symptom of the schism which had existed in the Church universal for a long time. Even after 1054 the conscious expression of the schism had not kept up with the fact. In the eleventh and twelfth centuries, examples indicate that some Greeks and Latins considered their two churches to be in complete union. During the Frankish occupation of Greece and Cyprus, this friendly relationship was readily demonstrated. While representatives of both churches looked upon their differences as minor and trivial,[1] by the end of the twelfth century and well into the thirteenth, economic and political clashes and a deeper exposure to one another's beliefs engendered a deep and vehement hatred.[2] On Cyprus the events of the eleventh, twelfth, and thirteenth centuries made both Latins and Orthodox fully aware of the many ecclesiastical differences which separated them.

Cultural, as well as linguistic, differences among the various groupings of Christendom had always existed. One of Christianity's greatest attributes was the ability to adapt itself to the culture, language, and attitudes of various peoples and nationalities. In time, however, these differences became magnified by both Orthodox and Latins on Cyprus until they finally became the core of heated controversy.

One of the key areas of doctrine which separated Latin from Orthodox was the Latin innovation and addition of the phrase *filioque* to the Nicene-Constantinopolitan Creed of the First and Second Ecumenical Synods (325 and 381 A. D., respectively). With this innovation the Latin creed reads: " . . . the Holy Spirit . . . which proceedeth from the Father and the Son." The Eastern Church rejected this addition both from an historical point of view, as well as a doctrinal one. A number of Eastern theologians spoke about the Holy Spirit as proceeding from the Father and the Son, as did Saint Augustine (d. 430), Saint Leo I (Pope 440-61), and Saint Gregory the Great (Pope 590-604). But those expressions never affected the text of the Creed which was treated both by West and East as a settled issue.[3] The central issue was whether the Church of Rome, by virtue of its own power, could change an article of universal orthodox belief, as defined by a supposedly infallible Ecumenical Synod, to make the article more intelligible; the *filioque* controversy centered on the validity of this argument.[4]

In the East, Saint Gregory of Nyssa (ca. 335-95) was the key figure in formulating theological opinion when he postulated that the Holy Spirit proceeds from the Father *through* the Son.[5] Before him Theodore of Mopsuestia (ca. 350-428) denied the *filioque* clause,[6] while Maximos the Confessor argued that any misunderstanding was due to the linguistic poverty and inadequacy of the Latin language. The procession of the Holy Spirit was understood to mean, claimed Maximos, that it proceeded *through* the Son.[7] These expressions, however, did not affect the text of the Creed affirmed and ratified by the first four Ecumenical Synods and accepted by both East and West. The alteration of the Creed occurred some time in the sixth or seventh century in Spain probably by mistake, for the Spanish Church had few men of learning in those early centuries. Most likely, those who first introduced the *filioque* clause thought that they were using the original version and had no intention of challenging the authority of the Ecumenical Synod.[8] This tradition spread north, and in the eighth century entered the theological tradition of the Frankish Church. Carolingian theologians began interpreting the *filioque* in the strictest and most literal of terms. Although a few popes (Hadrian I and Leo III) opposed it, by the ninth century the *filioque* had become a permanent tradition in the West.[9] This tradition became the object of attack by the patriarch Photios, whose opposition to the Latins included a strong attack on the hierarchy of the Western Church. In one of his homilies, Photios, probably for the first time, suggests that the "shepherds" of the West were heretics:

Why have slanders and calumnies against the clergy been the subject of my narration? Why? So that you may learn, my beloved, and be mindful that for one bishop to devise harm and weave deceits against another of Christ's bishops is an invention of heretics who have risen against the Son of God, our God, in indiscreet anger.

It is the outgrowth of men who have received in their souls

so great a seed of impiety; the wrong deed of men who have defiled the Christian faith. When you see them making a show of their abuse to our bishops and priests, remember their teachers and examples set for them, and recognize them for what they are, and of what they are made; for "by their fruits," the Lord's saying proclaims, "you shall know them" (Matthew 7.16). To know this is to avoid the imitation of them whose irreverence has already disgusted you, but who still may draw you in little by little because you have not completely severed your relationship with them. Is the shepherd a heretic? Then he is a wolf, and it will be needful to flee and keep away from him ... Is the shepherd orthodox? ... Then submit to him, since he governs according to the standards of Christ.[10]

As the issues of the procession of the Holy Spirit became the object of heated debate in the next several centuries, the Orthodox began to adapt to the reasoning of Patriarch Photios in their attitudes toward the Latins.[11] The Latins in turn, in total ignorance of the history of the addition of the *filioque,* actually charged the Byzantines of Constantinople with the crime of having *deleted* the phrase from the Creed.[12] By the beginning of the twelfth century, the *filioque* was an issue over which there was bitter controversy. Each side retreated from an earlier, more moderate, position, took up an extreme one, and firmly believed that it was defending orthodoxy against heresy.

The cultural and political division between two halves of the Christian world resulted in religious differences which were to become crucial by the eleventh century. A reading of the canons of the Quinisext Synod in Trullo (691-92), called by Emperor Justinian II, significantly reveals this cleavage in religious traditions that had already emerged.[13] One of the chief areas of friction was the issue of married clergy. In the Christian Church and in the Byzantine Empire there had always been married clergymen as well as celibates. Until the sixth century bishops might be married, but from that century

Church canons stated that bishops must be celibate. In the West, however, the Spanish Council of Elvira (ca. 300) insisted that the clergy, bishops, priests, and deacons, renounce cohabitation with their wives and the desire to have children.[14] In the East a married man was eligible to be ordained bishop, but no clergyman already ordained was allowed to marry. Canon Six of the Quinisext Synod allowed marriage after ordination up to the rank of subdeacon;[15] Canon Thirteen condemned the Latin practice of obligatory celibacy, or separation of wives of deacons and priests. Canon Forty-eight stipulated that even a married priest might be ordained bishop if his wife agreed to enter a convent.

Although there were other religious theological differences distinguishing the Latin Church from the Greek (fasting on Saturdays, confirmation administered by a priest immediately following baptism, etc.), the most serious one, especially from the eleventh century on, was the Latin use of unleavened bread (*azyma*) for the Holy Eucharist.[16]

Leavened bread (*enzyma*) was used in the early Church.[17] In the West the use of unleavened bread was first recorded in the writings of the Venerable Bede in the eighth century.[18] Until the eleventh century the sources say little of the use of unleavened bread in the West. In the eleventh century Patriarch Michael Keroularios initiated a formal attack upon the Western practice of the use of unleavened bread. He ordered Archbishop Leo of Ochrid to draw up a treatise defending the Orthodox usage and attacking the Latin innovation.[19] Cardinal Humbert answered Leo of Ochrid with a letter written on behalf of Leo IX, who, it seems, became aware of the letter. Humbert defended the Latin usage and attacked the Orthodox practice.[20] Humbert also composed a treatise in answer to a work by Niketas Stethatos, a Byzantine monk, [21] who attacked the Latin form of worship. The issues involved, which were major items of conflict after the eleventh century, consisted of the following: the Latin omission to celebrate the Liturgy of the Presanctified Gifts on fast days in Lent; the arrogant custom of the Latin priests of shaving off their beards; the continued practice of compulsory celibacy; the question of divorce, which the Latins forbade but the Orthodox allowed on certain grounds; the doctrinal point of Purgatory, which seemed to the Orthodox to be all-inclusive.[22] To profess to know what God in His infinite wisdom might choose to do with the souls of the departed was irreligious and scripturally unfounded, they thought. Most fathers, however, believed that the souls not actually condemned to hell at the second coming of Christ might yet be considered unworthy to be admitted at once into eternal bliss, and that prayer (memorials) might aid such souls in achieving this end.[23] The Latins questioned two Orthodox practices in the celebration of the Eucharist: the use of the "zeon," warm water mixed into the chalice with the wine to be consecrated; and more important, the *epiklesis,* the invocation of the Holy Spirit, without which, the Orthodox maintained, the change or *metousiosis* of the elements could not be effectuated.[24] All of these points were utilized by Latins to subjugate further the Greeks on Cyprus in the thirteenth century.

In their struggles against the various powers which opposed their authority in the West, a careful reading of the documents shows that the Roman pontiffs from the eleventh century gradually created an absolute interpretation of their primacy. In the ninth century when metropolitan bishops were trying to reform the Church and attempting to supress the Caesaropapism of the German Emperors, the popes were able to thwart these efforts by means of an ecclesiastical doctrine which made the pope head of the Church. This doctrine implied temporal sovereignty over the Christian universe. Because of the schism the Roman pontiff was no longer just a patriarch of the West, nor did he hold merely a "primacy of honor" within the perspective of a "pentarchy of patriarchs" (Rome, Constantinople, Alexandria, Antioch, and Jerusalem) which they had accepted *de facto* if not *de jure* at the time of the ecumenical synods. After the tenth century they solved the problems which they faced from a Western perspective and within a framework of purely Western institutional

developments. Cardinal Humbert's attitude in Constantinople in 1054 is obviously an extreme example of this new situation, but it is still a valid illustration of the outlook dominant
at that time in Rome. Against the attacks of the Byzantines
on the Latin rite, the Roman legates had no arguments other
than violent condemnations of the traditional Byzantine
customs: "removal" of the *filioque* from the Creed, the clergy's
wearing of beards, using unleavened bread in the Holy
Eucharist, etc.

Although these were extreme examples, the later popes did,
in fact, seek to assimilate the East into the institutional and
liturgical framework of Latin Christendom. These efforts
culminated in Innocent III's approval of the election of a Latin
patriarch of Constantinople after the city had fallen to the
crusaders in 1204. The documents of this early period verify
one fact; in the mind of the Latins of that time, Roman and
Latin Christendom coincided and a natural phenomenon with
the Church universal.[25] Ritual became less and less an issue,
while doctrine was treated more seriously. The Orthodox constantly had recourse to the idea of a synod for union, and on
most occasions the papal answer was that it was sufficient to
conform to the decrees of the Roman Church.

Such was the case when the Orthodox prelates on the island
of Cyprus, according to the demands of the *Bulla* or *Constitutio
Cypria* of 1260 were already swearing fealty to the Latin archbishop. The Cypriot Greek Church had theoretically yielded
her independence to the pressure of the Latins and had lost
her position within the Orthodox Greek communion. As late
as 1412, at the Synod of Constantinople, Joseph Bryennios
crushed Cypriots' hopes of restoration within the Orthodox
communion of churches. He condemned the Cypriots as unfit
for communion with the Orthodox Church because they had
submitted to Latin coercion. To prove their complete subser-
vience to Rome, he quoted from the oath taken by the Cypriot
bishops and described the ceremony of consecration. The
Latins and Cypriots were one body. The pope, and no other,
was head of this body. To condone such a state of affairs,

argued Bryennios, would set too dangerous a precedent for other Orthodox churches.[26]

The Dominican Angelo Calepio, vicar-general of the province of Terra Santa, wrote about the siege and capture of Nicosia and Famagusta by the Turks (1570):

> This was, indeed, a punishment and act of justice upon the Greeks in this kingdom, many of whom, while they were under the rule of Latin Christians, abhorred the limpid water of the Holy Roman obedience, and despised the life-giving stream of its head; for as these Greeks preferred to be subjects to that gangrened limb, the patriarch of Constantinople, because he and his fellow Greek patriarchs, especially the patriarch of Jerusalem, when the poor Cypriot merchants and pilgrims went into their churches, held aloof from them, considering them excommunicate, because in Cyprus they gave their allegience to the Latins; and saying the same in even stronger terms to the Greek bishops of Cyprus because they were elected to the Royal Latin Council, and confirmed by the Latin bishops; hence this ignorant people began to nourish a secret hatred against the Latins, as persons excommunicate and accursed.[27]

During the six centuries which separated the patriarchates of Photios (858-67; 877-86) and Gennadios Scholarios (1454-56), Byzantium and Rome never ceased to consider one another as parts of a single Christendom between which communion could be restored with relative ease. The schism was accepted as established fact, but not as a permanent situation. During each century several attempts were made to end it.

The history of thirteenth-century Cyprus shows the result of *sacerdotium's* asserting its authority over *imperium* in the West, when the popes had, in fact, become the sole spokesman for Western Christendom. The cloud that hung over Cyprus was never dispelled from the minds of the Orthodox; it even possibly blinded them to the brighter aspects of Roman history, affected all religious and cultural contacts between East and West, and raised problems that were further to poison the relations between the two churches on Cyprus. If an accomplished and sincere union in the interest of mutual benefit had been made, the fate of the Latin states in 1291 after the fall of Acre might have been different. However, when King Henry II of Cyprus, son of Hugh, needed the help of Cypriots against the Muslims, the Orthodox bishops refused to encourage the Orthodox faithful to support the king, his two hundred knights, and five hundred footsoldiers. In the spring of 1291, the Latins retained about six towns from Antartos to Athlith along the coast of Syria opposite Cyprus. In August of 1291, the complete extinction of the Latins' colonies occurred. Pope Nicholas IV attempted to kindle fraternal relationships between Latins and Greeks in order to unite against the common enemy,[28] but after the death of Nicholas IV, the ideals of the crusade gradually faded. With the pope's death, the possibility of a European occupation of the East also died.

9. Bellapais Abbey — 13th century

10. Kykko Monastery — 11th century

11. Hagia Napa Monastery, 14th-15th century

Chapter Six

BYZANTINES AND LATINS: POLITICAL DIFFERENCES

From the earliest times the Byzantines in the East had always acknowledged that the see of Rome held a certain position of honor in the synods of the Church. Two apostles, Peter and Paul, had founded the Church in Rome; its bishops had acquired a remarkable reputation for orthodoxy and provided a useful court of appeals in matters of faith. The Byzantines long remained respectfully sympathetic to the bishopric of the ancient capital of the empire, referring to it as the "elder Rome — palaia Rome." No one doubted the supremacy of Rome in the pentarchy of patriarchs, for the Twenty-eighth canon of Chalcedon had merely declared (to the satisfaction of Byzantium, at least) that the privileges of the bishops of Rome and Constantinople were equal. The canon had also stated that ecclesiastical precedence should be given to the "elder Rome."

The primacy of Rome was, therefore, an accepted part of the imperial scheme of things. The Byzantines could question the necessity for a Holy Roman Empire in the West, but they could not conceive of a Church without Rome as first among equals.[1]

In the fifth century Pope Gelasios addressed a long letter

to Emperor Anastasios, setting forth at length the principles which should be followed in adjusting the relations of the Church and the Imperium. Gelasios' theory is important in clarifying the relations of lay and clerical leaders. Many times in the thirteenth century churchmen alluded to it:

> Before the coming of Christ there were justly and legitimately those who were both king and priest, such as Melchizedek; and Satan imitated this among among the unbelievers. Hence it was that the pagan emperors held the office of Pontifex Maximus. The true and perfect king and priest was Christ Himself, and in that sense in which His people are partakers of His nature they may be said to be a royal and priestly race. But Christ, knowing the weakness of human nature, and careful for the welfare of His people, separated the two offices, giving to each its particular function and duty. Thus the Christian emperor needs the ecclesiastic for the attainment of eternal life, and the ecclesiastic depends upon the government of the emperor in temporal things. There are, then, two authorities by which chiefly the world is ruled, the sacred authority of the prelates and the royal power; but the burden laid upon the priests is the heavier, for they will have to give account in the divine judgement, even for the kings of men. Thus it is that the emperor looks to them for the means of his salvation, and submits to them and to their judgement in sacred matters. The authority of the emperor is derived from the divine order, and the rulers of religion obey his laws; he should, therefore, more zealously obey them. If the bishop is silent when he ought to speak for the divine religion, he will run great danger, and so also will he who condemns this authority instead of obeying it. If the faithful owe obedience to all priests, how much more do they owe it to the bishop of that see which God has set over all priests.[2]

In the mind of Gelasios, two authorities, that of the priests and that of the princes, ruled the world. A Christian society entrusted the spiritual and the temporal power to two different orders, each deriving its authority from God, each supreme in its own sphere, and each independent of the other. Furthermore, Gelasios insisted that, although independent, neither could escape contact and relationship with the other. The king was subject to the bishop in spiritual matters, the bishop to the king in temporal matters. Gelasios was cognizant of the fact that there can be no absolute separation of Church and Imperium, but he made no attempt to determine the bounds of the jurisdiction either of the Church or the Imperium, or to say when they overlapped. He did maintain that the Imperium must acknowledge the Church as a separate and independent source of legislation, and jurisdiction as a vital and imperative principle of Christian life and action.

The policy outlined by Gelasios was not an innovation. He merely systematized and formulated the principles which the Empire had consistently followed since the time of Constantine. His statements, however, were of considerable importance because they were, at the same time, an exposition of doctrine and a program of action which laid the groundwork for succeeding popes. Between the fifth and eighth centuries, the old system, gradually eroding, began to give way to the new — the feudal system. With the rise of feudalism a new set of difficulties again confronted the Church in the West in the attempt to adjust its relations with Byzantium. Both Church and Imperium had suffered severely from the social and political paralysis which had settled on Europe as a result of the influx of the Germanic groups. An amalgamation of peoples and an assimilation of ideas and institutions followed the völkerwanderung. The coronation of Charlemagne indicated not only a revival of the Roman Empire in the West, but also a union.

The barbarian invasions of the West and their consequences magnified the prestige and authority of the papacy in Western Europe. So, too, the occupation of Egypt, Syria, and Palestine (and with them, Alexandria, Antioch, and Jerusalem) by the

Arabs greatly added to the authority of the patriarchate of Constantinople in the Eastern world. By the eighth century authority in the Church narrowed in practice to the bishops of Rome and Constantinople. The papacy and Byzantium assumed roles which they had fully developed by the time of the crusades. By the eighth century the pope, slighted, neglected, and offended by an emperor who espoused iconoclasm, ceased to regard himself obligated to that emperor and turned for support to the Frankish monarchy. Before this time, developments had not shown any close relationship between the Franks and the papacy. The journey of Pope Stephen II in 753-54 to the Frankish kingdom was decisive. The purpose of the journey was to use the Franks' genuine veneration for Saint Peter and his office to emancipate the papacy from the framework of the imperial government. Prior to this trip, the Frankish ruler, Pepin, had established closer contact with the papacy with results he himself could hardly have forseen. When Pepin made a *coup d'état* against the king, Childeric III, Pope Zacharias, drawing on Gelasian doctrine, sanctified Pepin's seizure of power. Stephen's pretext for invoking Pepin's help was the alleged threat of the Lombards to Rome. The spurious "Donation of Constantine" would serve as the means to justify the claims of the papacy, finally emancipated from Byzantine imperial control.[3]

From the papal point of view, the coronation of Pepin's son Charlemagne on Christmas Day, A.D. 800, carried the idea of supremacy to its logical conclusion. By crowning Charlemagne the pope transformed the Western Imperium into equal dignity with that of the East. The title-deed to dispose of the imperial crown was plainly derived from the "Donation of Constantine," under which the pope allowed the Byzantine emperor to wear the crown which actually was the pope's. Pope Leo III "re-transferred" the imperial crown from Byzantium to Rome. The coronation was the final and solemn act by which Rome again became the center of the Roman Empire. The existence of two Roman emperors, each being the "Lord of the World," was impossible. According to the papacy, an emperor of the Romans could only be a Roman, an adherent to the Roman Church. He must acknowledge the supremacy of the Roman Church — the very point strenuously denied by Byzantium.

The opposing views between East and West first came into serious collision in the ninth century with the so-called Photian Schism. The patriarch Photios, perhaps the greatest statesman, philosopher, and theologian that Byzantium ever produced, believed that the papacy was in grave error when the *filioque* clause was added to the creed of the Ecumenical Synods and, worse still, when it encouraged its missionaries to propagate this false doctrine among the innocent Slavs. In this context, the singular and remarkable figure of Pope Nicholas I (858)867) appeared. Because Nicholas briefly inherited the Carolingian legacy, Hincmar claimed that Nicholas elevated himself to the emperorship of the whole world.[4] Nor did Nicholas hesitate to scorn the Byzantine emperors for their ignorance of Latin. He told them that they were not emperors of the Romans. The Roman Empire was in the West for Nicholas. Consequently, he inherited the difficulties inherent in this position which was consistent with the decisions formulated at the Council of Frankfort in 794. At this council, the Frankish king, independent of pope and emperor, not only dictated dogma for the Church with respect to icons and iconography, but also stated clearly that the Frankfort Council was universal. The council implied that the Byzantine Basileus had been replaced by a new universal council of the West which claimed to direct the entire Church. The Frankish king, speaking as *pontifex maximus,* prevented the papacy from dealing ecclesiastically with Byzantium,[5] for the decrees of the Council of Frankfort did not apply to the Byzantine Patriarchate. These differences became forcibly clear when the two spheres of influence later collided in Bulgaria. The *filioque* became the issue which sowed seeds of discord over the centuries. The effects of this encounter, generally known as the "Photian Schism,"[6] reflect the prejudice employed to damage the Byzantine position in the eyes of the West.

The conflict over the Creed took place in Bulgaria where Frankish orthodoxy, in the person of Formosus, bishop of Porto, a representative of Latin Christianity, confronted Greek Orthodoxy centered in Constantinople. Since Frankish liturgical uses were prevalent in Porto, Formosus naturally introduced them into the newly converted country. Because Nicholas rejected the election of Photios and the authority of the emperor, antagonistic feelings toward Rome prevailed in the imperial capital. In his "systatic profession of the faith," Photios had committed himself in the traditional fashion to the procession of the Holy Spirit from the Father. According to the Eastern Orthodox, additions to the Creed questioned the authority of the Ecumenical Synods and the Fathers.[7] In all his writings, Photios never mentioned offences against himself, only against the "Symbol of Faith."[8] How could the papacy claim to be the supreme head of the Church when it was so manifestly in error? The "Photian Schism" was settled, but only to the temporary satisfaction of both parties. These issues exerted a powerful influence on the minds of the Byzantines. They added to the theory of the *translatio imperii* by creating a new picture of the ecclesiastical as well as the political leadership of Constantinople. The Byzantines began to argue that Rome, through malpractice and heresy, through unauthorized tampering with the Creed and traditions of the Ecumenical Church, had forfeited even the few honorary privileges left to it by Constantine. By the authority of the Twenty-eighth Canon of Chalcedon, the see of Constantinople had become heir to those privileges.[9]

Beginning with Otto I in 962, the Saxon emperors came to Rome to be crowned and based their universal claims on the appeal contained in the Roman tradition. On such an occasion the Frankish innovation finally found its way into the Roman liturgy, according to Berno, an eye-witness.[10] The change came in 1014 at the coronation of Henry II, the Saxon successsor to the imperial mantle. Since Henry was from the North, he was naturally accustomed to the Frankish-Germanic liturgical practices which had permeated the West since the time of the Carolingians and which were common in his kingdom. He was surprised to hear the mass with the *filioque* omittted. On Henry's insistence the Creed containing the *filioque* became part of the Roman mass with the blessing of Benedict VIII (1012-1024). From this time, popes appointed by the Saxon emperors were not commemorated in the diptychs of Constantinople.[11] This practice has continued to the present day in the East. In the days of the crusades, the Byzantines primarily considered the Western Church as heretical. Byzantium, shorn of much of its glory, turned to Photios in his role of theologian as the great upholder of the Orthodox faith and tradition.

When Humbert of Silva Candida and Frederick of Lorraine came as legates to Constantinople in 1054, the Latin bull of excommunication so completely ignored the facts that the Latins accused the Orthodox of having omitted the *filioque* from the Creed.[12] What was the real purpose of the embassy? The mission was not an evangelical embassy to Emperor Constantine IX and Patriarch Michael Keroularios; neither did it intend to explain the supremacy of the papacy and return the "misguided" Greeks to the obedience of Rome.[13] The purpose of the mission moreover was not to anathematize the Byzantine Church nor to offend the emperor. Humbert had two letters from Pope Leo IX. One was a harsh letter to the patriarch, the other a warning to the emperor. The legates, ignored by the patriarch, stayed in one of the imperial palaces for at least three months. The papal embassy had as its major purpose the conclusion of an alliance between the papacy and the emperor against the Norman invaders of southern Italy. The Normans in Italy were as much an embarrassment to the papacy as they were to Byzantium. In 1053 they captured the pope. Since the pope was a Norman prisoner, the Byzantines should have conducted negotiations as secretly as possible. However, these negotiations were completely overshadowed and forgotten as a result of the ecclesiastical controversy. The personalities of Humbert and Keroularios violently clashed, and diplomacy became impossible. As G. Ostrogorsky states, "neither of the two hesitated to tear down the veil concealing the age-long latent differences."[14] Emperor Constantine, who might have controlled the situation, was unable to retstrain the volatile temper of his patriarch. The events of 1054 are clearly a refutation of the charge of Byzantine Caesaropapism. The religious dispute disrupted the friendship between pope and emperor. The latter even presided over a dispute between the papal legates and members of the Orthodox clergy in the hope of promoting a reconciliation. However, all the dogmatic and liturgical issues raised during the "Photian Schism" became battle-cries once again. The final dramatic moment came on July 16, when Humbert entered Hagia Sophia immediately before the Divine Liturgy and placed a bull of excommunication on the altar. In the words of A. Fortescue:

> It was Saturday, July 16, 1054, at the third hour (9:00 A.M.). Hagia Sophia was full of people. The priests and deacons are vested, the *prothesis* (preparation) of the holy liturgy has just begun. Then the three Latin legates walk up the great church through the Royal Doors of the Ikonostasis and lay their bull of excommunication on the altar. As they turn their backs they say: "Videat Deus et iudicet."[15]

Fortescue's interpretation is misleading. The affair of 1054 was a symptom and not the origin nor the cause of the schism which manifested intolerance and ill-feeling. From Humbert's point of view the Byzantine Church was a part of the Roman Church that had gone astray. He accused the Byzantines of being "prozymite" heretics or *fermentacei*.[16] According to their own traditions, the Byzantines were correct. According to Humbert, the Byzantines, in following their own traditions, were different from Rome and therefore wrong.

Patriarch Michael relpied to the excommunication by burning all copies of the bull and anathematizing its authors. He was careful, however, to avoid implicating the papacy, since Pope Leo IX had died soon after the legate's arrival in

Constantinople. The patriarch and the people of Constantinople believed that a papal legate had deliberately insulted them and their faith.[17]

During the next few years, relations between East and West slightly improved. After Patriarch Michael Keroularios was deposed in 1058, the Latin churches in Constantinople were re-opened. The Norman threat to southern Italy was a concern to both the papacy and Byzantium. This common concern paved the way for a temporary truce. The emperor re-opened the Latin churches in Constantinople, and Empress Theodora corresponded with Pope Victor II. Frederick of Lorraine, now Pope Stephen IX, dispatched a new embassy to Constantinople in 1058 to cement the alliance which his own legation had failed to secure.[18] However, Stephen died and his legates turned back before they left the shores of Italy. Pope Nicholas II managed to secure and agreement with the Norman leader, Robert Guiscard. This alliance in 1059 paved the way for the Norman conquest of Bari in 1071, the last remaining Byzantine possession in Italy.

By that time, the Byzantine Empire, ruled by the civil aristocracy of the capital, found itself unable to defend its lands even closer than Italy. They were unable to cope with the double invasion that swept the empire — by the Patzinaks from across the Danube and by the Turks from the heart of Asia Minor. In 1065 the Seljuk Turks entered Armenia and advanced to the Eastern provinces of Byzantium. In 1071 they defeated and captured Emperor Romanos IV in a battle at Manzikert. The loss of Bari and the defeat at Manzikert in the same year indicated the condition of the empire. In 1071 Jerusalem and the Holy Sepulchre also passed into Turkish hands for the first time.

These desperate circumstances minimized the ecclesiastical differences between Byzantium and the papacy. Leaders in all parts of Europe, including Byzantium, considered the papacy as the only power able to restrain the Normans and the Patzinak Turks. After the fall of Manzikert, the new emperor of Byzantium, Michael VII, opened negotiations with both the Normans and with Gregory VII, the new pope. Gregory opened a new page in the history of East-West relations. Church and Imperium assumed new dimensions which presaged the crusades.

Not content with the conquest of southern Italy and Sicily, Robert Guiscard planned an expedition across the Adriatic to invade the Balkans and Greece. Michael VII made three attempts to forestall this disaster by drafting an alliance with Guiscard. In 1074 this alliance established Guiscard as the defender of the empire's frontiers in the West. To cement the alliance, Guiscard betrothed his daughter to Constantine, the emperor's son. At this time Guiscard and Pope Gregory VII were in dispute. The pope's words and actions showed that he was prepared to follow a more vigorous policy of reform than that of his predecessors.[18] Michael VII and Gregory VII conducted negotiations independent of any Byzantine negotiations with the Normans. Michael obviously did not comprehend the conception of the papacy espoused by Hildebrand, any more than Constantine had understood that of Humbert, Hildebrand's friend. The alliance between Michael and Gregory confirmed the contention of J. Strayer, who views such alliances as "public power in private hands."[19] In essence, the deterioration in the external situation of the empire induced the Byzantines to try to establish better relations with the papacy. Gregory's letters indicated that he was even laying the plans for a church-directed crusade to the East, under his personal leadership.[20] Michael knew that an alliance with the papacy was an immediate necessity. The Normans might invade Byzantium at any time, and the Turks were a perennial threat to Asia Minor. Michael was ready to resort to the union of the churches of Rome and Constantinople to receive military assistance from the papacy. He was the first emperor to offer ecclesiastical union in return for military aid,[21] a procedure which continued for the next four centuries and which culminated in the Council of Florence in 1439. The correspondence between Michael VII and Gregory VII has not survived.[22] When Gregory sent the patriarch of Venice to

Constantinople in 1073, the patriarch reported that the situation in the East was critical. Pilgrimages to the Holy Land had flourished under the rule of the Fatimids. The pope was particularly distressed to learn that Turkish occupation of Palestine might block the route through Anatolia.[23] In February of 1074, Gregory wrote to William, Count of Burgundy, and asked him to lead an expedition, first to Italy to pacify the Normans, and then to Constantinople, where the Christians "are urging us eagerly to reach out our hands to the in succour."[24] Gregory proposed a holy war against the infidel. Runciman considers Gregory's plan a "stroke of imaginative statesmanship." A holy war, already occurring in Spain and Sicily, should also take place in Asia. He himself would lead the expedition. In December of 1074, Gregory reported to Henry IV of Germany that 50,000 men would march to Constantinople under his command. During a synod in Constantinople, he, as supreme pontiff, would receive the submission of the Greeks. From Constantinople the expedition would reach "as far as the sepulchre of our Lord."[25] In his correspondence with Henry IV, Gregory mentioned the main reason for his expedition to the East:

> . . . Because the Church of Constantinople, which disagrees with us about the Holy Ghost, desires to come to an agreement with the apostolic throne.[26]

In 1080 Gregory convinced Robert Guiscard to become his ally. When the Normans prepared to invade the Balkan peninsula, Gregory gave his support to the enterprise. He excommunicated Nikephoros III Botaniates, a member of the military aristocracy of Byzantium, who had deposed Michael VII to become emperor in 1078. The excommunication seemed superfluous since the breech between East and West, brought about as a result of the schism of 1054, meant that every succeeding Byzantine emperor was also under the ban of excommunication. Although the real Michael was living in a monastery, Guiscard produced a Byzantine monk who pretended to be the deposed emperor. Gregory accepted the imposter. On July 24, 1080, he wrote to the bishops of Apulia and Calabria that all the faithful of Saint Peter should aid in reinstating Emperor Michael, "unjustly overthrown," and that all men able to fight should pay allegiance to the emperor and Guiscard.[27]

In 1081 Alexios Komnenos became emperor by deposing Nikephoros III in yet another civil war. When the Normans crossed the Atlantic and invaded the Balkans with the blessing of Gregory, the "Norman pope," Alexios supported Henry IV. The pope, who had become so interested in the defense of Eastern Christians, was now their hated enemy.[28]

One of the most disasterous chapters of the relationship between Church in the West and Imperium in the East began with the reign of Alexios Komnenos. He was not only an efficient soldier, but also an astute statesman. He knew that immediate past history suggested that the emperor and the patriarch must co-operate for the good of the empire.

When Guiscard invaded the empire in the Spring of 1081, Alexios was encountering the Seljuk Turks at Nikaia, but he soon reached an agreement with them. At this time he also negotiated with Henry IV of Germany and tried to create dissension among the Normans in southern Italy. Through a treaty with the Venetians, he obtained naval support in return for commercial privileges (1082). While Henry IV marched upon Rome to resolve his differences with Gregory VII, a revolt erupted in southern Italy against the authority of Guiscard, who then returned to Italy and left his son, Bohemond, to wage war with the emperor. When Guiscard suddenly died in 1085, the Norman invasion of Greece temporarily ceased. Pope Gregory also died in the same year. As a result, relationships worsened not only between Constantinople and the papacy but also between the papacy and the Normans.

Four years later, the Frenchman, Odo of Lagery, became pope and took the name of Urban II. Under Gregory VII, he was canon, archdeacon, and then cardinal-bishop of Ostia. Relationships with the East improved under the leadership of Urban

II.[29] In 1089 Urban lifted the excommunication that Gregory VII had imposed on Alexios. In return Alexios re-opened the Latin churches of Constantinople, and the diptychs once again contained the pope's name. Count Roger, Robert Guiscard's brother, assured the pope that there would be no further Norman invasions of Greece. Alexios welcomed this new gesture of friendship from the papacy and then called a synod in Constantinople in September of 1089. The patriarchs of Constantinople and Antioch, eighteen metropolitans, and two archbishops attended. Alexios presided over the meeting. The proceedings of this synod are important because they reflect an attempt to heal the schism on canonical grounds.[30] Since no official records of the separation of Rome from Constantinople existed, the synod tried to re-establish provisional communion between the two churches even though the Greeks evidently objected to the questions of the *filioque, azyme,* and the primacy of the papacy. The synod then made the following compromise:

> Urban II should first of all send to Constantinople his profession of faith. If the pope's profession of faith were found to be sound, if he accepted the seven Ecumenical Synods and the local synods which the latter approved, if he condemned the heretics and the errors which the Church condemned, and if he respected and accepted the holy canons which the Fathers of the Church had adopted at the Sixth Ecumenical Synod, then his name would be put back in the diptychs of the Church of Constantinople. This arrangement was to be temporary, pending the holding of a synod in Constantinople which was to regulate and eliminate the differences between the two churches. This synod was to be held within eighteen months after the receipt of the papal profession of faith and was to be attended either by a papal delegate or by the pope himself. The synod urged the patriarchs of Alexandria and Jerusalem to accept this compromise.[31]

At the same time, the patriarch of Constantinople, Nicholas III, wrote a friendly letter to Urban II explaining that the Latins were free to worship according to their customs in Byzantium; hopefully, the Greeks in Italy would have the same freedom.[32]

The reconciliatory policies of Alexios were not very popular in the East. Sources reveal conflicting evidence concerning whether Urban sent the required profession of faith or accepted the invitation to this synod.[33] Yet Alexios did succeed in removing some of the differences which separated him from the papacy, whose help he desperately needed, in addition to mercenary troops. In 1090 the Patzinaks reached the walls of Constantinople from the Danube frontier and besieged the city by land and sea. In 1091 Alexios administered a crushing defeat on the Patzinaks; at the same time he asked for military aid from the pope.[34] In earlier centuries, Anatolia had been the breeding ground for the empire's native troops. The Seljuk Turks now occupied this area. Alexios, therefore, depended on the western European market to provide the East with knights and soldiers. Anna Komnene wrote that her father attempted to engage a mercenary army. He sent letters to various authorities in the West. She indicates that in 1091 he awaited a mercenary army even from Rome.[35] Robert the Frisian, count of Flanders, sent five hundred mounted warriors together with one hundred and fifty horses. While Urban II was busily establishing the papacy as "the recognised centre and head of Christendom,"[36] Alexios, believing that Constantinople was the center and capital of Christendom, welcomed the mercenaries who had come to defend the capital and its eastern frontiers. This opinion differed from the actual situation of disunion between East and West and prompted Geoffrey Baraclough to reject any "feelings of unity" during the Middle Ages. He speculated:

That unity, if it existed at all, was either spiritual (and as such was represented by the Church), or it was material (and as such was represented by a supra-national empire);

but from either point of view it is a conception hard to reconcile with the known facts.[37]

Although the situation in the East improved by 1095, Alexios continued his quest for help against the invading Seljuks. He sent two emissaries to the Council of Piacenza in March of 1095. The council dealt with means of furthering the reform programs of Gregory VII and of dealing with "schismatics."[38] Many prestigious people were present at the council.[39] Urban gave his wholehearted support to the requests of the Byzantine embassy and urged men to give aid to Emperor Alexios and the Eastern Church. At this council, Urban stressed the theme of Christian brotherhood. If the Christians of the West aided their brethren in the East, the Eastern emperor, who was already on good terms with the pope, would urge Christians of the East to acknowledge the supremacy of the Rome. Urban preached outside the city to a crowd too large for the Cathedral of Piacenza. Bernold relates that Urban exacted a vow of obedience to the papacy.[40] At the Council of Clermont a few months later, Urban completed the work, which he had begun at Piacenza. In November of 1095, Urban preached his great sermon which summoned all of western Christendom to fight the Holy War.[41] Within months several armies journeyed to Constantinople. Despite the fact that Alexios asked for help from the West and from the pope, he never expected a crusading army. His appeal was specifically for mercenaries to fight with the Byzantine armies, not for mass migrations from West to East. Alexios reassured the populace of Constantinople that Westerners would rid the Empire of foreign barbarians and would not interfere in the Christian affairs of Byzantium.[42] According to Gibbon:

In some Oriental tale I have read the fable of a shepherd, who was ruined by the accomplishment of his own wishes: he had prayed for water; the Ganges was turned into his grounds; and his flock and cottage were swept away by the inundation. Such was the fortune or at least the apprehension of the Greek emperor, Alexios Komnenos.[43]

The fact that four of the eight leaders of the First Crusade were Normans undoubtedly did not encourage Alexios. Yet, both sides took measures to preserve the peace, and at religious services they exchanged the kiss of peace. When Raymond of Toulouse reached Byzantium, the chonicler, Raymond of Aguilers, wrote:

> We believed that we were in our homeland (in Patria Nostra) since the feelings we had were those of brotherhood and love which we knew that the Emperor Alexios and his vassals had for us.[44]

When Alexios sent mercenary troops to lead the armies from the West, cordial relations changed. Byzantine mercenaries killed two barons; the mercenaries forced Adhemar of Pur, the papal legate, to leave the main force after they had wounded him; they attacked Raymond himself. Apparently the mass influx of Western foreigners into the Byzantine mainland was promoting misunderstanding between Byzantines and Westerners. Seeing both churchmen and crusaders carrying weapons especially shocked the emperor's famous daughter, Anna Komnene. She wrote:

> The Latins do not have the same idea of a priest as we have. . . . The barbarian Latin participates in the divine mysteries while at the same time girding his shield on his left hand and grasping his spear in his right. He gives communion in the divine Body and Blood while he looks on slaughter and becomes a man of blood himself.

Such observations underline the essential differences between Westerners and Byzantines. Urban clearly required that the crusaders restore to Byzantium all territories wrested from the Turks. The crusaders ignored the admonition, although they acted in the name of the pope. If the crusade was a papal and not an imperial project, then the "soldiers of Christ" could only perform God's work under the universal head of all Christendom, the pope.[46] The Byzantines could not understand the conception. To the East, the emperor was in fact the head and defender of all Christendom. The armies under his command, whether Byzantine or Latin, were performing God's work by preserving the frontiers of the empire. Reconciliation of opposing viewpoints was improbable. The later course of the crusades, culminating in the disaster of 1204, clearly showed that West and East differed fundamentally on the order of the world. Later controversies on Cyprus would do little more than enlarge this difference and alter its direction.

The eleventh century began with a flourishing empire in the East and a weekened and ineffectual papacy in the West. The century ended with a powerful papacy in the West and an empire struggling to survive in the East.

Most historians agree that the Second Crusade was an almost total failure.[47] Bernard, the great proponent of the crusade to the East, voiced his shock at the outcome of the expeditions:

> We all know that the judgements of God are true; but this judgement is so deep that I could almost justify myself for calling him blessed who is not offended thereafter.[48]

One positive aspect of this Second Crusade was that it did not attack Constantinople. The emperor at this time was Manuel Komnenos. Byzantium was very weak militarily, and dissension existed in the army. The German emperor, Conrad III, threatened Manuel Komnenos with at attack on Constantinople if no shipping facilities were at the emperor's disposal. Conrad, experiencing disasters in Asia Minor, made an alliance with Manuel.[49]

Several sources explain why the crusaders did not attack Constantinople and other areas of Byzantium.[50] Odo de Deuil, whose chronicle is obviously prejudiced yet very detailed, demonstrates that a significant division of opinion about the

Byzantines existed within the French army. In February of 1147, the first of several recorded debates occured at Etampes, where Louis VII was making arrangements for the march. Apparently one day a heated debate among the French leaders arose about an offer by King Roger II of Sicily, the hereditary Western enemy of Byzantines, to transport the crusade by sea from Italy. Little is known of the arguments employed by the anti-Greek faction except that they cited previous writings, possibly chronicles or speeches, as well as their own experience that the Byzantines were dishonest and deceiving.[51] Odo de Deuil, who was king's chaplain, agreed with their views. He expressed angry disappointment when he had to record that Louis and the majority of the barons decided to avoid an entanglement with Roger II and go overland through Byzantine territory. In his opinion, the king was unwisely putting trust in a people addicted to "deception."[52] Unfortunately, the chronicle gives no information about those favoring cooperation with the Byzantines and, in effect, avoiding encounters with the Normans.

Soon another division of opinion erupted in the army. Emissaries of Manuel were awaiting the French king at Ratisbon (Regensburg, on the Danube at Bavaria) to make arrangements for the transit of the army through Byzantine territory. The emissaries informed the French barons that they must take two oaths: first, that the crusaders were not to take any of the emperor's territories; second, that they should restore to him any of his former possessions which they might gain from the Turks. The first oath aroused no controversy. Even the anti-Byzantine faction considered this demand quite proper. Everyone, however, was adverse to taking the second oath. The emissaries settled for the first oath alone with the promise that at Constantinople they would negotiate further about the second.[53]

Because it stands as a prologue to later relations between Latins and Byzantines, crusaders and churchmen, the division of opinion among the barons concerning the second oath is significant. The anti-Byzantine faction led by Godfrey, bishop of Langres, was unwilling to return any territory to Manuel unless the French received compensation. More moderate barons were willing to compromise. They merely wanted Manuel to define precisely what territories he regarded as his, "lest the obscurity of his proposal excite future litigation."[54] The moderates won the day, for although no one refused to take the second oath, the assembly tabled the question until the two rulers would meet and personally confer over the issue. Manuel did not bring this issue up again until the army had left Constantinople and had crossed to Asia Minor.

The two factions now became distinct. Their division would persist to and beyond Constantinople, even to the remote island of Cyprus years later. In Bulgaria the army found supplies short and the rate of exchange unfavorable. Other problems became acute in these strange lands. Both factions gave different reasons: the one blamed the Byzantines; the other, the German crusaders who were preceding them along the route and "who plundered everything."[55] The anti-Byzantine faction included religious issues in its grievances. Byzantine priests reportedly purified altars and sanctuaries after Latin priests had celebrated mass in them and required the rebaptism of Latins before marriage to a Byzantine. Coupled with these reports came the news that the Byzantines were "heretical" in their tradition of celebrating the Liturgy and in their beliefs concerning the procession of the Holy Spirit. Odo de Deuil then justified the violent acts against the Greeks as being both valid and necessary.

> For these causes they (i.e., the Greeks) had incurred the hatred of our men, for the knowledge of their error had spread abroad even among the laymen. On this account they were judged not to be Christians and our men concluded that slaughtering them was of no account. It became more difficult to hold them back from pillage and plunder.[56]

In fact, perhaps Odo exaggerated the charges a little, since

Louis VII welcomed religious processions which came out to greet him from the Greek villages. Even when he heard that Manuel had concluded a truce with the sultan of Ikonion and that an advance party of French crusaders was fighting with the emperor's troops in the city, Louis still agreed to enter the city with only a few of his barons to confer with the emperor. When they met, they exchanged the kiss of peace; when they parted, they did so as "brothers."[57]

During the army's encampment outside the walls, Bishop Godfrey of Langres sought to give the crusade another objective. He spoke to the assembled leaders of the army emphasizing the military weaknesses of the city in detail and proposed a plan for an easy seige of the city as well as of the whole Byzantine Empire. Godfrey went to counter the feeling of amity between Louis VII and Manuel. He argued that Constantinople was not even a Christian city.[58] The moderates fell back on more concise and familiar ground. The Byzantines were Christians; they, too, fought the pagans in defending the Holy Sepulchre. If the case were otherwise, the pope would have informed the king. Odo's summary depicts the philosophy of the anti-Byzantine faction:

> It is certainly true that the king recently conferred with the pope and that he was not given any advice or command concerning this point. He knows, and we know, that we are to visit the Holy Sepulchre and, by command of the supreme pontiff, to wipe out our sins with the blood or conversion of the infidels. Instead of this, however, we may now attack the richest city of the Christians and enrich ourselves, but in so doing we must kill or be killed. If, therefore, slaughtering Christians wipes out our sins, let us fight. Furthermore, if harboring ambition does not harm our dead, if on this journey it is as important to die for the sake of gaining money as it is to maintain our obedience to the supreme pontiff and our vow, then wealth is welcome; let us expose ourselves to danger without fear of death.[59]

In spite of Odo's admonition, the moderates spared Constantinople at least for another crusade, although Manuel did succeed in establishing suzerainty over the Latin crusader states which turned eventually to the emperor for protection from the Turks. The French army departed to Asia Minor. This eastward movement was the result of rumors, probably circulated by Manuel, that the German crusaders ahead of them were pillaging and conquering the Turks. Louis guaranteed the security of Manuel's eastern territories and continued his journey. The intention of the anti-Greek faction was to conquer Byzantine territory. The reply of the moderates, in contrast, was one of ideology and practical necessity; they needed Greek supplies and Greek guides through Asia Minor: "We are speeding against the pagans. Let us observe the peace of Christians."[60]

Evidence shows, however, that Louis VII did not wish to divert the crusade: first, he had family and diplomatic ties through Eleanor of Aquitaine with Raymond of Antioch, who was not on good terms with Roger II;[61] secondly, as the moderates had reminded Godfrey at Constantinople, Louis had conferred at length with the pope before the crusade had left Europe. The crusading policy of Eugenius III did not emphasize the reunion of churches as did that of Urban II: yet, he was more an issue of conscience to Louis VII than it was to the pope and the churchmen. Perhaps the king's original intention to go on crusade came from a bad conscience about his own gross breach of Christian obligations at the siege of Virty some years earlier. Louis visited a leper colony at Paris. He attended mass and other religious ceremonies during the march.

When the French crusaders returned home, unrest existed in France. Conflicting ideologies prevented the crusaders from conquering Byzantium and the East. St. Bernard, Suger, and Peter the Venerable added their voices to those churchmen who demanded a new crusade.

In Germany, Frederick I Barbarossa and his son, Henry VI, were also planning a crusade to remove the Byzantine stumbling block in the nebulous plans for Western domination of the East. Henry VI acquired the Norman kingdom of southern Italy and Sicily by marriage to Constance, the only surviving child of King Roger II. The papacy had stifled his father in his ambition. At the Diet of Regensburg, Frederick I Barbarossa and his son Henry made final arrangements for the march east on April 23, 1189 — Saint George's Day, a feast and saint's day in the East and the West. According to the Latin source, Ansbert,[63] the German army, one hundred thousand strong with a core of many knights, and with purses bulging with money, began the trip east. The leaders of the German Church and the German aristocracy directed the expedition. The bishops of Liege, Wurzburg, Passau, Regensburg, Basel, Meissen and Osnabruck, to whom were later added the archbishop of Tarentaise and the bishop of Toul, were among the leaders. In March 1190, after gaining as allies the sultan of Ikonion, the Serbians, the Bulgarians, and the crusaders crossed the Dardanelles straits.

A further threat to Byzantium took place in July 1189, when Frederick crossed the Balkans and Peter the Vlach offered aid to him in any plans against Byzantium. He promised Frederick 40,000 Vlach and Cuman archers for an attack on Constantinople, scheduled for the spring of 1190. That spring, however, Frederick reached an agreement with Isaak and decided not to attack Constantinople, since he was more anxious to proceed with the Crusade across the Straits than to delay in "Romania" and appease the lust of empire for somebody else. Although the danger of a Vlach-Crusader alliance had passed, in the summer of 1189 Isaak undertook an expedition against the Vlachs who were ravaging Byzantine territory. The Vlachs, defeated the imperial army at Sredna Gora. Isaak, says Niketas Choniates,[63] was like a honeycomb with bees buzzling all around it. The situation became acute as Isaak divided his army between the military leaders. He based himself at Varna and Anchialos, from which the Vlachs had withdrawn, and in the summer of 1190, near Philippolis, he attacked the Vlachs and the Serb zhupan, who had destroyed

Scopia. Again, the enemy caught Isaak's forces crossing the Morava River into south Servia and killed many soldiers. Isaak, nevertheless, passed Nish and moved across the Sava to a rendezvous with his brother-in-law, King Bela of Hungary. After having a conference with him and after planning joint action against the Vlachs, Isaak returned to Constantinople via Philippolis. Isaak appointed his cousin, Constantine Angelos, governor of Philippolis with the title *strategos,* and for a while he kept the Vlachs at a distance. Soon, Isaac found fault with him because Constantine Angelos fancied himself as emperor.[65] The Vlachs had feared Constantine Angelos. With this threat removed, they waged war once again and defeated the Byzantines. In 1195 Alexios Angelos, Isaak's brother, captured Isaak. He took command of the army and dethroned and blinded his brother Isaak. Eight years later, when the Latins arrived during the Fourth Crusade, Isaak was briefly rescued. Alexios III Angelos disbanded the army, allowing the Vlachs and Cumans to invade Byzantine territory. The emperor countered by sending his son-in-law, the sebastocrator Isaak, to lead another army. He, too, fell into a trap; the enemy destroyed his army and captured him near Serres. Isaak soon died in captivity; and Ivanko, a Vlach, who had killed Asen, the ruler of the Vlachs, became an ally of the Byzantines and of Alexios, the emperor. Ivanko fought diligently against his fellow Vlachs, a welcome change for Byzantium and Alexios III. The seriousness of the situation in Macedonia and Thrace, Niketas Choniates wrote, was indicative of the empire's need for allies, more so than any "commemorative inscription or historical writing."[66] Ivanko, so useful to the Byzantines for this brief period, eventually deserted, and the Vlachs and Cumans again began raiding Byzantine territory. Russian mercenaries, however, saved Constantinople.[67]

At that time, the young Alexios, son of the dethroned Isaak Angelos and nephew of Alexios III, had fled to the West to enlist sympathy and aid for his imprisoned father. When he returned, he had with him the forces of the Fourth Crusade. Niketas Choniates is the main source concerning the Vlach-

Cuman incursions from 1185 to the Latin diversion. Except for Albert's references to the negotiations between Frederick Barbarossa and the Vlach leaders, other sources reveal little. Choniates wrote about the semi-independent rulers — Chrysos, Ivanko, Kamytzes, and Spiridonakis — all of whom helped the Byzantine cause. Choniates also noted the revolt of Balkan peoples led by the Vlachs, Peter and Asen, and later by their brother Ioannitsa.

The whole chronology of events is important. The succession of military victories of Peter and Asen over the Angeloi Byzantine emperors made an impression on Innocent III. In 1199, the pope began corresponding with the Vlach leaders, and much of this correspondence survives.[68] In his first letter, written during the last two weeks of December 1199, Innocent III addressed his correspondent as "the noble man Ioannitsa," who achieved victories over the Byzantines by the grace of God. According to the pope, God had rewarded the Christian humility of Ioannitsa. The pope noted his devotion to the Latin West and the Roman Church. He explained in his letter that Ioannitsa's devotion to the Apostolic See, rather than to Constantinople, was in the best tradition since his ancestors had originally come from a noble Roman line. Innocent further informed him that he was sending the envoy Dominic, the protopresbyter of the Greeks at Brindisi, who should be accorded all the proper respect of a papal legate and who would be the first of many ambassadors to visit the Vlachs. These envoys of the pope would strengthen him and there would exist a continuous tie with Rome.[69] The letter responds to one from a Vlach leader informing Innocent that the Vlach-Bulgarian princes were ready to leave the Greek fold and enter the Roman. In 1202 Ioannitsa answered Innocent. The papal register notes that the letter of Ioannitsa was translated from Bulgarian to Greek and then to Latin. Ioannitsa described himself, according to the Latin version, "Caloiohannes Imperator Bulgarorum et Blachorum,"[70] and thanked the pope for his letter to him and his late brothers, Peter and Asen, who had unsuccessfully tried to communicate with the pope.

They now wished that the Roman Church accept them and crown them in the same fashion as the 'emperors of antiquity,' such as Peter the Bulgarian whom the Byzantines acknowledged as 'emperor' in 927. Finally, Ioannitsa assured the pope that he would accord due honor to the high ranking legates from the Holy See.[71] On November 27, 1202, Innocent replied to "Caloiohannes, Lord of the Bulgarians and the Vlachs," referring to the correspondence of popes Nicholas (858-67) and Adrian (867-72) with the king of the Bulgarians, Boris (852-89), who had been baptized with Emperor Michael III as his godfather by proxy. The pope sent Latin priests to convert Bulgaria in the ninth century. The Bulgarians soon found it to their advantage to drive all the Greek priests from Bulgaria. This turn of events strainded the relationships between Rome and Constantinople. Now, Innocent wrote, he would sent a chaplain to Ioannitsa and the Bulgarians. The chaplain had the authority to ordain priests and consecrate bishops. He also was to investigate the Bulgarian procedures and regulations of administration and then recommend any changes to the pope. In closing, the pope reminded Ioannitsa of the Roman origins of his people and of their affiliation to the see of Rome.[72] The original Latin of the pope's letter is very explicit, and one should study it closely. In 1199 several years prior to the Fourth Crusade, the Roman Church under Innocent III was closing in on the Eastern Empire through the Bulgarian kingdom — literally at the front door of that empire, a march of only one or two days from the Golden Horn. In particular, he planned to model the Vlacho-Bulgarian Church after the Latin Church.[73] He wrote a similar letter to Archbishop Basil, metropolitan of Zagora, as well as to a 'prince' named Bellota who had requested that the Latin Church admit him and his family.[74] These letters reveal that obedience to Rome was a prerequisite for any negotiation. Ioannitsa requested that the pope send the patriarchal staff and anything else necessary to change the status of Archbishop Basil from "primate" to that of "patriarch." He also asked for holy oil since Bulgaria was converting to Rome. Prior to this time, Constantinople had sent the holy oil to Bulgaria for its religious ceremonies. This oil was used in the sacrament of confirmation, a sacrament of the Church in both the Eastern and Western traditions. The oil or holy *myrron* was prepared every Holy Thursday at Constantinople and sent for use to all affiliate archdiocese and churches. In addition, Ioannitsa requested that the pope mediate in the boundary dispute between himself and the king of Hungary. As an acknowledgement of the primacy of Rome, Ioannitsa would send gifts: "examita dupplatria: et Cupam aurem et yperpeorum libras quattuor, et scutellas argenteas tres et gradale argenteum."[75] On October 15, 1204, Leo, Cardinal priest of Santa Croce, a legate of the Holy See, arrived in Tirnovo, annointed Basil on November 7, and crowned Ioannitsa king on the next day.[76] This final act converted Bulgaria to the papacy, the event preceded the disaster of the Fourth Crusade.

The crusaders assaulted the city of Constantinople in July 1203. They restored Isaak Angelos and crowned his son, the young Alexios. They sacked the city in April 1204. Count Baldwin of Flanders and Hainaut became the emperor of the established Latin Empire. The siege of Constantinople, its sacking, and the formation of the Latin Empire in the Greek East created a new situation between the kingdom of Ioannitsa and his immediate Latin neighbors, who were also under the pope. Ioannitsa immediately established a relationship with crusader armies. In the spring of 1204, before the second capture of Constantinople and the formation of the Latin Empire, Ioannitsa, in the words of the contemporary chronicler, Robert de Clari:

> . . . sent word to the high barons that if they would crown him king, so that he would be lord of his land of Vlachia, he would hold his land and kingdom from them, and would come to their aid to help them take Constantinople with all of a hundred thousand men. . . . When the Latins heard this, they said they would consider it, and when they had taken counsel, they came to a bad decision; for they

answered that they cared nothing for him nor for his help, but he should know well that they would hurt him and do him harm if they could. This was a very great mischance and a very great misfortune. Now when he had failed with them, he sent to Rome for his crown, and the apostolic see sent a Cardinal to crown him, and so he was crowned king.[77]

Ioannitsa then wrote to the pope and requested help at this time. The Vlachs and the Cumans established diplomatic relationships. The effort to gain the friendship of Latin crusaders and to form an alliance with them — a move encouraged by the papacy — was no more succesful than the establishment of the fateful Latin empire at Constantinople. In April 1205, Ioannitsa captured and killed Emperor Baldwin. He wrote to the pope that he had tried to reach a friedly agreement with the Latins. They insisted that he return to the Empire the lands which the Cumans had seized by force. Ioannitsa felt that this territory was his; these lands once belonged to his ancestors, and he would fight the crusaders in the name of the pope.[78]

The events described on preceding pages showed the weakness of the Angeloi dynasty and the greed and hostility of Byzantium's Latin enemies. This antagonism contributed to the fundamental change in the character of the Empire, resulting in the breakdown of central authority. The pattern in the West was very consistent. Innocent offered indulgences to the crusaders who recovered the vassal state of Sicily from Markwald in 1199.[79] Innocent declared that Christians who did not adhere to the Latin West, and the Church were "worse than Saracens" because they stood in the way of the recovery of the Holy Sepulchre.[80] H. Pissard maintains that this precedent set the stage for succeeding popes to direct a crusade against any rebelious city or leader who opposed the papacy. Honorius III preached a crusade against Pisa; Gregory IX preached one against Ezzolino da Romano and another against the city of Viterbo: a crusade was preached against Simon de Montfort as a rebel against the Church's vassal, Henry III of

England; Martin IV preached a crusade against Peter of
Aragon in 1282 after the Sicilian Vespers; Boniface VIII waged
a holy war against the Colonna family; John XXII, against the
Visconti of Milan. Pissard mentions that the pope's charge of
"heresy" could be made all the more easily because anyone
who failed to submit to the Church after a year of excommunication was suspected of heresy.[81]

Historians have conjectured several reasons for the failure
of the crusades. They have often empasized political and
military causes, but they have glossed over — even ignored
— the religious, economic, social, and intellectual causes. This
oversight indicates that the study of Byzantium itself has been
too long a neglected area of Western history. Now that the
darkness is gradually lifting, one sees that in the East, the
history of the Empire was much more than a chronicle of palace
intrigues, internal revolutions, theological controversies, con-
claves and ritualistic ceremonies which historians viewed as
trivial. The Fourth Crusade offers an opportunity for historians
to observe how people or rulers attempted to solve problems
peculiar to the history of the High Middle Ages and to see how
the characters of human beings and the accidents of history
which confronted them determined the course of events. These
events involved the establishment of an empire not only in Constantinople but also in other places. The history of Frankish
Greece begins with the Fourth Crusade — an attempt to unite
Europe and the East in the interest of temporal and ecclesiastical gain. After an existence of half a century, the Latin
empire of Constantinople also failed. Nevertheless, the East
remained full of Latin settlements. Venice retained the essential portions of her colonial empire in the Levant, Negropont
and Crete, and the strong citadels of Modon and Coron; her
patrician families kept most of their signories in the Archi-
pelago,[82] as did the other Latin states in Greece which were
products of the crusade.[83]

Hostility to the crusade arose following the Fourth Crusade.
No longer could a pope bring to bear the great force of public
opinion against a schismatic ruler in the East. No longer could

a pope depend on the stength of a reluctant king against the infidel.[84] No longer could a pope enforce his claims to be the supreme arbiter in temporal as well as spiritual affairs in the interest of Christian unity.[85] Even Louis IX could not depend upon spontaneous enthusiasm to bring recruits for his planned crusade. He resorted to subterfuge to induce his court to take the cross. Of all the sources of strength which the crusade had offered, only the tithe remained, and that fell to the mercy of the monarchs who did not hesitate to confiscate it during a national emergency.[86] Even taxation for a constantly postponed crusade fell into fiscal abuses which lasted to the Reformation.[87]

The Fourth Crusade was the beginning of the end, for it signalled the gradual disappearance of a great military force ready to defend the interest of theocracy. Without the zealous support of masses of Christians ready to sacrifice their lives for other-worldly ideals of the Church, the national states soon threatened the power of the papacy. Darkness emanated from a disillusioned Europe at the time of Michael Palaiologos' solemn entry into Constantinople on August 15, 1261, which marked the fall of the Latin Empire. Once and for all, the course of these events, the ideology of a united Christendom between Latins and Greeks had diminished. Caught in the throes of this struggle was Cyprus, a shining jewel in the Mediterranean, which closely tied its history of change, adaptation, and development to the changes which were taking place in other areas of mediaeval life. The legal institutions of the crusades reached the virtual limit of development on the island of Cyprus. After this time crusading institutions were clearly in stasis; predicatably, their subsequent history after Cyprus was one of gradual decay.[88]

12. Monastery of Apostle Barnabas

13. Monastery of St. Neophytos the Recluse — 12th century

14. Giuliana Gate, new Famagusta Gate

NOTES

CYPRUS PRIOR TO THE FOURTH CRUSADE

1. N. Iorga, *France de Chypre* (Paris, 1931), pp. 16-17; Sir George Hill, *A History of Cyprus*, 4 vols. (Cambridge, 1940-1952), 1, pp. 315-16.

2. The earliest Western authority on this subject is Paul the Deacon (end of the eighth century), *Hist. Miscella*, PL 95.1049; see also Hill, *Cyprus*, p. 184.

3. An "Akritic ballad" was the popular poetry of the time. The poems were either blank or rhyming, but in monotonous fifteen syllable verse. See K. Pharmakides, *Κύπρια ἔπη μετὰ σημειώσεων καὶ σχολίων* (Leukosia, 1926), pp. 88-96, for a detailed analysis of these epic poems.

4. For a comprehensive history of this see, see J. Hackett, *A History of the Orthodox Church of Cyprus* (London, 1901), pp. 318-19.

5. See H. Magoulias, *Byzantine Christianity: Emperor, Church and the West* (Chicago, 1970), p. 45, for a comprehensive picture of this event against the background of the Iconoclastic controversy.

6. Sir R. Storrs, *Orientations* (London, 1943), p. 470.

CYPRUS IN THE THIRTEENTH CENTURY

1. See Sir F.M. Powicke, *King Henry III and the Lord Edward* (Oxford, 1947), p. 171.

2. René Grousset, *The Epic of the Crusade*, trans. Noël Lindsay (New York, 1970), p. 200.

3. This Imperial Chrysobull can be found in G. Tafel and G. Thomas, *Partitio Regni Graeci*, in *Urkunden zur altern Handels — und Staatsgeschichte der Republik Venedig* (Vienna, 1856-57), 1, pp. 114-24. Louis de Mas Latrie, in *Histoire de l' Ile de Chypre sous le règne de la maison*

de Lusignan, 1, *Histoire jusqu'à 1291* (Paris, 1861); 2, p. 4, note 2, shows that there were Latin merchants at Lemesos in 1191 and Amalfitani merchants in Cyprus in 1168.

4. William of Tyre, 18, 10, in *Recueil,* 1, p. 835.

5. The Armenian version of Michael the Syrian, *Documents Arméniens,* 2 vols. (Paris, 1869-1906), 1, p. 350, in *Recueil,* says that Renaud's motives were two: first, that the Greeks ill-treat the Franks in Cyprus; second, that they encourage the Turks to kill Armenians.

6. Anna Komnene, *Alexiad,* Collection Byzantine de l' Association Guillaume Bude, ed. Bernard Leib, 3 vols. (Paris, 1937-45), 1, 13; (trans.), E. R. A. Sewter, *The Alexiad of Anna Komnena* (Baltimore, Maryland, 1969), pp. 90-91, pp. 272-73.

7. Hill, 1, pp. 304-06.

8. See also Stevenson, pp. 58-59.

9. William of Tyre, *Lib.* 12, 100. n. 22, as quoted in Hill, 1, p. 304, n. 5.

10. See the interesting note on Koutzoventi Monastery in Hill, 1, p. 305, n. 1. Saint Neophytos came to this monastery in 1152.

11. See Hill, 1, p. 305, n. 3.

12. Isaak Doukas Komnenos was a son of a daughter of Isaak the Sebastokrator, brother of Manual I. For background on Isaak Doukas Komnenos, see Brand, *Byzantium Confronts the West, 1180-1204* (Cambridge, Mass., 1968), p. 55.

13. The wedding took place in the chapel of the fortress of Lemesos; then she was crowned Queen of England by John Fitz Luke, bishop of Erreux, who had the distinction of being the officiant to the only oversea's territory of England which was the scene of both the wedding of an English king and queen and of an English coronation.

14. See Hill, 1, pp. 317ff., and notes for different versions of the conquest.

15. Isaak's wife was a daughter of Thoros II of Armenia.

16. For details of Richard's stay and departure, see Merton Jerome Hubert, *The Crusade of Richard Lionheart,* a translation of *Estoire de la Guerre Sainte* (New York, 1941), pp. 85-107; *Itinerarium Peregrinorum et gesta regis Ricardi,* ed. by William Stubbs, in *Chronicles and Memorials of the Reign of Richard I,* 2 vols., Rolls Series (1867), 38, pp. 187-204; *Gesta Regis Henrici II,* ascribed to Abbot Benedict of Peterborough and edited by Stubbs, 49, 2, pp. 163-68; Hill, 2, pp. 31ff. For details of Isaak's capture and imprisonment, see Brand, p. 124.

17. De Mas Latrie, 3, p. 595. On Aimery's death the two crowns were

separated until 1269, when they were finally reunited in the person of Hugh III. In 1393 a third crown was added to these by the death of Leo VI, King of Armenia, whose next of kin was James I of Cyprus. Eighteen sovereigns of the House of Lusignan occupied the throne of Cyprus between 1192 and 1369; see Sir Harry Luke, *Cyprus* (London, 1957), p. 45.

18. At his death Aimery's revenues on Cyprus had risen to at least 200,000 byzants. (See *Eracles,* in *Recueil des Historiens des Croisades; Historiens Occidentaux,* 2, pp. 190-91). The *Chronique d' Ernou et de Bernard le Treserier,* ed. de Mas Latrie (Paris, 1871), p. 288, says that the annual revenue from lands in Cyprus was estimated at 300,000 white byzants. This is an interesting piece of evidence since, Cyprus, according to some sources, was destitute due to the quarrels between the secular and the ecclesiastical powers of the island. See pp. 119-20, n. 179, above.

19. De Mas Latrie, *Histoire,* 1, p. 122.

20. P. Jaffe, *Regesta Pontificum Romanorum* (Leipzig, 1888), 2, p. 620, no. 17329. See also J. LaMonte, "A Register of the Cartulary of the Cathedral of Santa Sophia of Nicosia," *Byzantion,* 5 (1929-30) 444, no. 2.

21. De Mas Latrie, *Histoire,* 1, pp. 123ff. The three were Paphos, Limassol and Famagusta. (See map, Appendix C.) De Mas Latrie, p. 125, relates that at first the funds for establishment came partly from public domains or from lands whose owners had abandoned them. Funds also came from rights and possessions of the casales (hamlets and villages) of Ornithi and Aphandia, as well as from tithes of the lands conferred upon the Church by the Holy See, such as Nicosia and its environs, the casales of Solia, Lapithos, Kythrea, Sivouri, etc., numbering about seventeen (LaMonte, p. 445, no. 3).

22. De Mas Latrie, *Histoire,* 1, p. 124. See also Pius Bonifacius Gams, *Series Episcoporum Ecclesiae Catholicae* (Graz, 1957), pp. 430-39. Gams' lists seem to confirm the fact that, indeed, the bishops of the other two sees are unknown. Gams only confirms that when Cyprus was seized in 1191, orders were received from Rome to move the capital from Constantia (Salamis) to Nicosia. Gams also mentions that in 1218, Symeon, the Greek archbishop, was to be subject to the Latin metropolitan archbishop. The bull of 1196, therefore, is the only source on which one can depend.

23. Eracles, 2, pp. 209-11. De Mas Latrie, *Histoire,* 1, p. 127, and *Chronique d' Ernou,* p. 303.

24. The translation reads "bishop," while the original Greek reads *proedros* which means "president," the status the Archbishop of Cyprus holds to the present day.

25. The metropolis of Cyprus, which was formerly called Konstantia,

when restored by the Emperor Justinian II was called by his name, New Justinianopolis.

26. Translated and edited by Percival, "The Seven Ecumenical Councils of the Undivided Church," *Nicene and Post-Nicene Fathers of the Christian Church* (Grand Rapids, 1956), 14, p. 383.

27. Percival, p. 235.

28. For an account of this story, see Greek translation and revision of Hackett, by Charilaos I. Papaioannou (Vol. 1, Athens, 1923; Vol. 2, Piraieus, 1927; Vol. 3, Piraieus, 1932), 1, pp. 40-42.

29. Papaioannou, 1, p. 41; Hill, 1, p. 278.

30. G. I. Konidares, *Αί μητροπόλεις καὶ ἀρχιεπισκοπαὶ τοῦ Οἰκουμενικοῦ Πατριαρχείου καὶ τάξις αὐτῶν*, Text and Forschungen, 13 (Athens, 1934). Also his *Ἡ θέσις τῆς αὐτοκεφάλου Ἐκκλησίας τῆς Κύπρου ἔναντι τοῦ Οἰκουμενικοῦ Πατριαρχείου κατὰ τὸν Θ.΄ καὶ Ι.΄ αἰῶνα*, 18 (Athens, 1943), pp. 135-46.

31. Konidares, *Αί μητροπόλεις*, p. 140.

32. Konidares, *Θέσις αὐτοκεφάλου*, pp. 135-36, 139, 142.

33. Konidares, *Θέσις αὐτοκεφάλου*, p. 141.

34. A. I. Dikigoropoulos, "The Church of Cyprus During the Period of the Arab Wars, A.D. 649-965," *The Greek Orthodox Theological Review*, 9 (1965-66) 256-58.

35. Konidares, in *Θέσις αὐτοκεφάλου*, p. 141, refers to the *Notitia* of Emperor Leo III which he dates in the period 733-746 and which refer to the bishop of Konstantia as the third metropolitan after those of Caesarea and Ephesos. In fact, the archbishop of Cyprus, Constantine, is referred to as bishop of Konstantia in the Acts of the Seventh Ecumenical Synod in 787 at Nikaia, which he signs after the metropolitan of Ephesos. There is a letter of the archbishop of Cyprus, Epiphanios, to Patriarch Ignatios in 870, whom he addressed as "Despotes" (a title which only a subordinate-in-rank would use). It seems, however, that these titles were used in addressing prelates of an autocephalous church, whose autocephaly still respected the rights of honor of the Ecumenical Patriarchate.

36. Justinian, *Codex Juris Civilis*, 1.3-35; G. Ostrogorsky, "Byzantine Cities in the Early Middle Ages," *Dumbarton Oaks Papers*, 13 (1959) 47-66.

37. Dikigoropoulos, p. 239; Hackett-Papaioannou, chapter 6.

38. Dikigoropoulos, pp. 239-40.

39. Hill, 1, p. 263. See n. 1, in which he cites the fact that Theodosiana or Theodosias is Neapolis, as proven by the *Life of Spyridon* by Theodoros, bishop of Paphos, ed. Papageorgios (Athens, 1901), Chapter 23, pp. 95ff.

Although Dikigoropoulos, p. 240, confirms that at the Ecumenical Synod of Chalcedon in 451 there was present a bishop of Theodosia, this writer has not found this name on any map of this or any other period which has been studied. For a more recent edition of the *Life of Spyridon,* see P. Van den Ven, *La Légende de S. Spyridon, évêque de Trimithonte,* Bibliothèque de Muséon 33 (Louvain, 1953) pp. 1-103.

40. See Hill, 1, pp. 270-71.

41. De Mas Latrie, *Histoire,* 1, p. 125.

42. *Gesta Innocentii III Papae,* in PL 214.123-25.

43. *The Gestes des Chiprois,* 514, in *Recueil: Documents Arméniens* 2, p. 818, describes Cyprus as a source of supplies: "mout rich et bone et bien plaintive de tous biens."

44. For precise distances between Cyprus and key places, see C.F.A. Schaeffer, *Missions en Chypre, 1932-1935* (Paris, 1936), pp. 1ff.

45. Cyprus was only at the mercy of Moslem invaders from the seventh to the tenth century. Many historians, for this reason, criticize Emperor Constantine Porphyrogennetos for including Cyprus in his list of Byzantine themes. J. B. Bury, in *History of the Later Roman Empire, 2,* pp. 340-41, says that, as a result, Cyprus could not be considered as a definite part of the Byzantine empire. Constantine Porphyrogennetos, *De Thomatibus,* 1. 15, as quoted in Hill, 1, p. 259. See also note, "The First Moslem Invasions of Cyprus," in Hill, 1, p. 326.

46. The most important product of the island was copper which was mined in antiquity in the foothills of Troedos and along the coastal districts from Farium to Soli (see map.). Cyprus exported copper as early as the second millenium B.C. Other products which made Cyprus a commercial center were iron ore, asbestos, ship-building, timber, olives, wine, etc. For details see the following works: C. V. Bellamy and A. J. Cullis, "Sketch of the Geology and Mineral Resources of Cyprus," in *Journal of Social Arts* (New York, 1924), pp. 624-47; R. Storrs and B. J. O' Brien, *Handbook of Cyprus* (New York, 1930), pp. 234-59. The etymology of Cyprus is uncertain, according to Hill, 1, pp. 82-83. One encounters *Kypros,* the name, for the first time in the eleventh book of the *Iliad,* in connection with the legend of Kinyras, and in the *Odyssey.*

47. Richard received 100,000 byzants. For a detailed discussion of the sale, see Hill, 2, pp. 67-69.

48. On November 22, 1197, he gave to Joscios, Archbishop of Tyre, the village of Livadi on Cyprus and exempted the produce of this village from

export dues. This procedure held true for all other exports from Cyprus to the church of Tyre. See de Mas Latrie, *Histoire,* 3, p. 606; see also LaMonte, p. 444, no. 7.

49. Stubbs gives an excellent appraisal of the reasons: "Within the feudal fabric itself, custom or perhaps principle, was more dominant than law . . . The kings lived, for the most part, the life of adventurers of knights-errant, playing their part in the defense of Christendom but still, like the great military orders and fragmentary principalities of Palestine, only as an isolated garison in the middle of a world out of which they were being gradually driven; no more, as Richar had hoped, an advance post in the great campaign by which the East was to be humbled before the West." Stubbs, *Seventeen Lectures on the Study of Medieval and Modern History* (Oxford, 1887), pp. 193-94.

50. J. L. LaMonte, *Feudal Monarchy in the Latin Kingdom of Jerusalem* (Cambridge, Mass., 1932).

51. The competitive arm of jurisdiction on Cyprus was the Court of Bourgeois or *Basse Cour,* organized under the viscounts (sheriffs) and acting as courts of law on a local level. Apparently, it also judged cases which involved nobles; Stubbs, *Medieval and Modern History,* p. 195. One recorded case which came before the *Basse Cour* was the sale of a house to the archbishop in 1292 by a canon of Nicosia. The transaction took place according to the custom of the *Assizes of Jerusalem,* the policy which Cyprus followed. The viscount of the city of Nicosia presided. De Mas Latrie, *Histoire,* 3, pp. 675-77; LaMonte, "Register," no. 106, p. 531.

52. LaMonte, *Feudal Monarchy,* pp. 256-57. The *Seneschal* was master of the court ceremonies and head of the financial administration. He convened and presided over the *Haute Cour,* and in military matters he represented the king in the king's absence. The *constable* acted as military judge and was supreme commander of the army and the mercenaries. The *marshal* was the lieutenant under the constable. He carried the royal banner in battle and distributed the spoils after victory. The *chamberlain* was the personal attendant of the king in his chambers and in the palace. He administered the oath to those who paid homage to the king. The *chancellor* did little more than draw up charters. He never achieved the prominence and importance which the office attained in the West in the thirteenth century. All chancellors were clerics.

53. Hill, 2, p. 54. The king chose him from among the knights, and he presided over the "courts of the bourgeois." Because Nicosia was the first and only headquarters for the viscount under the Lusignans, the district

of Nicosia became known as the *Visconté;* See de Mas Latrie, *Histoire,* 2, p. 110; 3, p. 495. Elizabeth Chapin Furber informs one that an official with the title of *Mathesep* assisted the viscount. The word derives from the Arabic *Muhtasib,* inspector of weights and measures, Furber, "The Kingdom of Cyprus, 1191-1291," *A History of the Crusades,* ed. Setton, 2, p. 620.

54. Wilbrandi de Oldenberg, *Peregrinatio,* published by J. C. M. Laurent, *Peregrinatores medii aevi quatuor,* 2nd ed. (Leipzig, 1873), and trans. Claude Delaval Cobham, in *Excerpta Cypria* (Cambridge, 1908), p. 13.

55. See R. L. Wolff, "The Organization of the Latin Patriarchate of Constantinople, 1204-1261," *Traditio,* 6 (1948) 41. See also LaMonte, "Register," 5, nos. 14 and 16.

56. See LaMonte, *Feudal Monarchy,* p. 52, and n. 1.

57. See Hill, 2, pp. 801-83.

58. LaMonte, *Feudal Monarchy,* p. 52, n. 2.

59. Potthast, 1, p. 245, no. 2865. In a letter dated January 13, 1213, the king, as one learns from the pope's letter, had sent the archdeacon of Famagusta to Rome to protest against what he regarded as capricious condemnation of the patriarch. The pope rebuked and threatened the king and directed the chapter to elect another archbishop, submitting their recommendation to the patriarch, the archbishop of Caesarea and the bishop of Acre.

60. O. Raynaldus, *Annales Ecclesiastici denuo excusi* (Cologne, 1773), an. 1213, as quoted in Harry J. Magoulias, "A Study in Roman Catholic and Greek Orthodox Relations on Cyprus," *The Greek Orthodox Theological Review,* 8 (1964) 77.

61. George Acropolites, *Georgii Acropolitae Opera,* ed. A. Heisenberg (Leipzig, 1903), pp. 29-30.

62. December 17, 1221 (LaMonte, "Register," No. 17); December 30, 1221 (de Mas Latrie, *Histoire,* p. 44; Potthast, no. 6748); January 5, 1222 (LaMonte, "Register," no. 18); March 8, 1222 ("Register," no. 20).

63. The articles are listed in Hill, 3, p. 1043.

64. The letter, dated March 8, 1222, is found in p. Pressutti, *Regesta Honorii Papae III* (Rome, 1895), 2, p. 35, no. 3750. Cf. LaMonte, "Register," p. 452, no. 20.

65. The letter is dated January 3, 1222. Potthast, no. 6755. De Mas Latrie, *Histoire,* 2, p. 45, gives the date as January 23, 1222. The queen of Cyprus at this time was Alice of Champagne, who was recognized as regent of the kingdom and guardian of her infant son, Henry I (1218-1243). The pope,

Honorius III, took the queen under his protection and ordered his legate Pelagius to do the same, Letter of July 12, 1218, in de Mas Latrie, *Histoire*, 3, p. 610.

66. A letter dated from September 14, 1222, and found in LaMonte,"Register," p. 453, no. 23, mentions that the four Greek bishops who, henceforth, would be subject to the Latin prelates, should now move from their residences at Nicosia, Paphos, Limassol and Famagusta, and relocate themselves at Soli, Arsinoe, Lefkara and Karpasso, respectively. The relocation was for no apparent reason, except to harass and subjugate the Greek clergy further.

67. Philip d' Ibelin was the younger brother of the Old Lord of Beirut (and the queen's uncle) with whom she agreed to share in the administration of the kingdom. The Latins granted extensive commercial privileges to the Genoese and to Philip (de Mas Latrie, *Histoire*, 1, p. 198; for the text of the diploma from *Gen.*, see 2, p. 39).

68. De Mas Latrie, *Histoire*, 2, p. 47; Potthast, no. 7458. In a letter Patriarch Germanos of Constantinople replied to the request for guidance, which the Cypriots addressed to him, with basically four complaints: first, that there should be only one archbishop, a Latin, who with his three suffragan bishops would have complete control of the island, since the Greek bishops would be completely subordinate to them and the Latin ordinaries of the districts in which they resided; second, the courts of the Latin ordinaries must ratify an appeals or decisions of the Greek bishops; third, no Greek elected to a position in his church should be allowed to take office without the permission of the Latin ordinary; fourth, upon his election, every Greek bishop should kneel before his Latin ordinary and do homage and swear fealty as vassal to lord, Hackett, pp. 83, 89ff.; Papaioannou, 1, pp. 115, 123ff.; de Mas Latrie, *Histoire*, 1, pp. 209-10.

69. De Mas Latrie, *Histoire*, 2, p. 47; Potthast, no. 7458. For a discussion of the sources concerning the exact date of this marriage, see Hill, 2, p. 88, note 3.

70. In 1472 a bull of Pope Sixtus IV concerning certain irregularities on the island, confirmed the validity of the four dioceses (de Mas Latrie, *Histoire*, 3, pp. 325-30; LaMonte, "Register," p. 522, no. 131.)

71. Magoulias, *Church Relations on Cyprus*, p. 80, quotes and translates this letter found in de Mas Latrie, *Histoire*, 1, p. 213.

72. Hill, 3, pp. 1047-1048, records also that the Synod took the advice and ordered the Cypriot bishops, including their Greek constituency, should refuse to do homage; however, it directed that in obtaining leave of the

ordinary to take possession of office or submitting decisions of appeal of their own bishops, they should yield.

73. Hackett, pp. 91ff.; Papaioannou, 1, pp. 126ff.

74. The patriarch's letter is quite significant historically, as it gives evidence of the official view of the Byzantines at this time against Latin Catholic inter-communion. The letter is reminiscent of the sentiments voiced with a vengeance in the letter of a Cypriot priest and cloistered monk, Neophytos, written in 1196 and found in Jean B. Cotelier, E. Cod. Reg. 2376, in his *Ecclesiae Graecae Monumenta* (Paris, 1681), 2, p. 460. The letter of Germanos was important since the pope appointed a commission of two Dominicans and two Franciscans to investigate the charges with the hope of bringing the two churches closer together. (Letter of May 18, 1223, in Sathas, p. 47; Hackett, p. 99; Papaioannou, 1, p. 137.)

75. Papaioannou, 1, pp. 120-31. "Narrative of the Thirteen Holy Fathers Burnt by the Latins of Cyprus" in Sathas, 2, pp. 20-39.

76. In a letter dated March 5, 1231, Pope Gregory IX (1227-1241) ordered the archbishop of Nicosia (Eustorge) to excommunicate heretic Greek monks who did not use unleavened bread in the performance of the sacrament of Eucharist. LaMonte, "Register," pp. 455-56, no. 28. (Note the retaliation to Germanos, who used the word "heretic" in describing the Latins.)

77. This example is further proof showing just how much Latin customs had penetrated into the Greek East.

78. The incident is one of many showing how this custom of "trial by fire" had penetrated in all of the Greek East. The famous incident of Michael Palaiologos, before he became emperor and while he was the youthful governor of the Thracian towns of Melnik and Serres, is worthy of note; see the contemporary historian, George Akropolites, 1, pp. 83-93; also Deno J. Geanokoplos, *Emperor Michael Palaeologus and the West* (Cambridge, Mass., 1959), pp. 21-24.

79. De Ecclesiae Occidentalis atque Orientalis Perpetuae Consensione (Cologne, 1648), p. 700; as quoted in Magoulias, *Church Relations on Cyprus* p. 84.

80. LaMonte, "Register," p. 463, no. 48. Cf. Potthast, 1, p. 920, no. 10868 which gives evidence of Pope Gregory's order to Eustorge to fill the posts of the recusant Greek clerics, who fled to Armenia, with Latins and to gain support of the secular and civil authorities toward this end.

81. For a thorough discussion on the alliance between Vatatzes and Frederick II, see Vasiliev, *History of the Byzantine Empire 324-1453* (Madison, 1952), pp. 526-30.

82. E. Berger, *Les Registres d' Innocent IV* (Paris, 1884), 1, p. 614, no. 4051. Compare the *Liber Augustalis or Constitutions of Melfi Promulgated by the Emperor Frederick II for the Kingdom of Sicily in 1231,* trans. James M. Powell (New York, 1971), for an understanding of the changes that Frederick II tried to effect. The effect on Cyprus was profound. This common body of law, compiled at the behest of Frederick, emphasized the shift in the structure of medieval society from localism to more centralized states. The problem of these states was uncertainty whether the monarchs could hold new states together. Frederick had squelched rebellions by the Muslim population and by the nobility, had negotiated with the clergy over disputed domains, and finally had defeated the papal army that had invaded his kingdom during the crusade of 1228-29. The establishment of his royal authority in that kingdom, based on the Constitutions of Melfi, was the same policy seemingly used on Cyprus; see Chapter 5 for elucidation.

83. This policy seems to be an extension of the policy of conciliation with the Greeks of Cyprus rather than coercion, which had thus far failed. The exemption granted in July 1243 to the Greek Basilian monastery of Saint Marguerite de Agro in the diocese of Nicosia, exempting it from tithe on the lands which it possessed and cultivated itself, showed an earlier sign of this policy. LaMonte, "Register," p. 464, no. 52. In the "Cartulary," a letter of January 25, 1245, sent to the patriarch of Jeruslem, instructed him "to protect the monks of Saint Marguerite de Agro from all molestation"; "Register," p. 465, no. 55.

84. Berger, 2, p. 134, no. 4769.

85. N. Gappuyns published an episcopal list of Cyprus in 1935 and published an episcopal list of Cyprus in 1935 and recorded the names of twenty-eight archbishops of the island from the foundation of the church by Barnabas, to the late twelfth century. Gappuyns took this list from the *Codex Sinaiticus* 989, cols. 20r-37r, and compiled it in *Le Synodikon de Chypre au XIII Siècle,* 2, 10 (Paris, 1935), p. 489.

86. The Latin prelate Eustorge had died on April 28, 1250, while at Damietta with Louis; Amadi, p. 200. *Chroniques d' Amadi et de Strambaldi; Collection de documents inédits sur l' histoire de France,* ed. L. de Mas Latrie (Paris, 1891).

87. The charge is in the eighteenth century collection by Mansi, *Sacrorum Conciliorum Nova et Amplissima Collectio,* 31 vols. (Florence and Venice, 1759-98), 26, p. 336.

88. The pope granted him permission through a directive on December 20, 1251. De Mas Latrie, *Histoire,* 2, p. 65, note 2; see also Berger, 3, p. 16, no. 5523.

89. Only a few confusing reports of him exist. Hackett suggests that he was archbishop of Nicosia in Sicily (p. 310, n. 2; Papaioannou, 2, p. 75, n. 2) as the account of Mansi, 24, col. 66, reads; "per eum (scil. patriarcham Graecorum) et Archiepiscopum Nicosiensem, et alios Graecos sui secum (i.e. with the patriarch) venerant, et alios archiepiscopos, et abbates Graecos de regno Siciliae . . ." Hill, 3, p. 1056, n. 1, rightfully questions whether this place in Sicily was ever an archepiscopal see. Cams justifies this question.

90. Mansi, 23, col. 1038.

91. Berger, 4, p. 381, no. 7338. Hackett enumerates the decisions of Pope Innocent IV to Cardinal Eudes, pp. 105-12; Papaioannou, 1, pp. 144-52:

1) The Greeks must adhere to Roman usage in the administration of the sacrament of Chrism or Confirmation. The use of cold or warm water in Baptism was immaterial for the validity of the sacrament.

2) Only the bishop was allowed to confirm according to Roman practice; thus the Greeks must discontinue the custom of administering the sacrament of Chrism (Confirmation) by the priest.

3) Chrism must now consist of balsam and olive oil, and the Greek bishops must consecrate it on Maundy Thursday. (The Greeks, instead of "balm," used forty different kinds of aromatic spices. They must discontinue this practice and adopt the Roman usage.)

4) He forbade the Greek practice of administering Holy Unction in the case of grievous sin in lieu of the satisfaction of penance.

5) The sick must receive extreme Unction.

6) The Greeks could continue to mix warm water in the wine of Holy Communion as long as they recognized that the kind of water used made no real difference; cold, hot or tepid.

7) He forbade the Eucharist consecrated on Maundy Thursday and reserved on the altar for the sick until next Maundy Thursday; the sacrament might be kept no longer than fifteen days.

8) The Greeks could celebrate the Liturgy according to their own tradition, but not after the ninth hour.

9) The Greek priests must finish matins before they celebrated the Mass (Liturgy).

10) The Latin ordinary must first examine candidates for the priesthood to see if they knew the canonical hours and the office of the mass in their proper sequences (secundum distinctionem temporum).

11) The Greeks must use only chalices of gold, silver, or pewter for the Eucharist. (Wooden chalices were in use up to the ninth century.)

12) Women were precluded from all ministrations of the Altar.

13) The Greeks could continue their practice of not fasting on Saturdays during Lent.

14) Married priests, as well as celibates, might hear confession and impose penances upon the constituents for their sins.

15) Bishops could use any cleric they deemed fit for the task of hearing confessions and imposing penances, as well as discharging other spiritual matters in their dioceses.

16) Divorced persons could not remarry. The Latin Church regarded remarriage as a mortal sin.

17) Greek bishops henceforth must conform to the Roman usage of conferring the seven orders; priest, deacon, sub-deacon, acolyte, exorcist, reader, ostiarius.

18) The Greeks must not condemn second, third, or even fourth marriages. (Hackett, p. 111, quotes a portion of the chapter of Nikephoros, Patriarch of Constantinople, and confessor; "He that enters into a second marriage is not crowned in the service; and, in addition to that, is warned not to receive the spotless for two years; and he that enters into a third, for five.")

19) The Greeks must accept the Roman concept of purgatory.

20) Anyone who died in mortal sin without penance as doomed to eternal damnation.

21) Baptized infants and saintly Christians who died went immediately to heaven.

22) Greek abbots and monks must strictly observe the monastic rules and ordinances set down by the Church Fathers.

92. LaMonte, "Register," p. 474, no. 89.

93. "Register," p. 474, no. 89. For a letter of Alexander, see also de Mas Latrie, *Histoire,* 3, p. 652. The account was probably satisfactorily settled since no record of any excommunication exists. Jean S. de Joinville never mentions Henry, although he mentions people and events of lesser importance; J. S. de Joinville, *Chronicle Histoire de Saint Louis, Credo, et Lettre à Louis X* ed. N. de Wailly; *History* ed. and trans. Sir Frank T. Marzials (New York, 1958).

94. See LaMonte, "Register," p. 474, no. 91, for the bull of Alexander IV dated July 3, 1260. This bull, also known as the *Bulla* or *Constitutio Cypria,* ruled on the status of the Greek Church and the Eastern jurisdictions. The Bulla came after Hugh had excommunicated Germanos and stripped his vicars of their functions. Germanos in turn had

excommunicated certain Latins. Germanos was called to Rome with "Nibon de Solia, Joachim de Carpasio, Mathias de Lefchars, Graecarum sedium Cypri episcopi"; Mansi, 23, cols. 1037-46. In LaMonte, "Register," p. 474, no. 91, read "Nilo of Solia" for "Nibon de Solia." The pope asked Cardinal Eudes, who was back in Rome, to mediate the dispute, since the cardinal was responsible for Germanos' investiture. Hugh's representatives in Rome defended him in the following ways:

1) The decisions of Cardinal Pelagius in organizing the Latin church of Cyprus had clearly defined that the kingdom of Cyprus could have only one ecclesiastical head, the Latin archbishop of Nicosia.

2) Germanos' decisions and rulings were invalid, therefore, as well as his election, since the suffragan bishops who elected him were also under excommunication at the time. Alexander, taking everything into consideration, published at Anagni, his residence, the historic *Bulla* on July 3, 1260. LaMonte, "Register," describes it as a regulatory measure, "providing for the supremacy of the Latins and subjecting Germanos, the Greek archbishop, Nilo of Soli, Joachim of Karpasso, and Mathew of Lefkara, Greek bishops, to the supremacy of Hugh, archbishop of Nicosia."

95. "Germanos was evidently regarded with great consideration by the papal authorities." Hill, 3, p. 1061. "Without prejudice (!) to any rights over Greeks enjoyed. . . Germanos was made completely independent (!) of the Latin archbishop and bishops, " ibid.

96. Hackett, pp. 114-23, and Papaioannou, pp. 154-64, confirm this form, found in Mansi. According to the *Bulla* or *Constitutio Cypria*, the Greek Church should conform to the following guidelines:

1. The Greek sees should remain at four with the Latin archbishop as the metropolitan of the island.

2. The Greeks must elect new members from the clerics in the diocese in which the vacancy occured. This election must have the approval of the Latin bishop of the diocese, who first must exact the "oath of the obedience." (See prescribed from above.)

3) Litigations must be decided as follows: the Greek bishop was to make the final decision in the ecclesiastical court when the litigation was between Greeks. Mixed cases (Latin and Greek) must go before the Latin bishop, who, in certain cases, had the right of censure over the Greek bishops.

4) Latin bishops would have the right and priviledge to visit all suffragan Greek dioceses. The Greeks would be responsible for collecting monies to offset the expenses for these visitations. (Apparently this practice continued at least until the middle of the fifteenth century. LaMonte registers

a letter dated April 4, 1547, of Brother Francis of Famagusta of the Dominican order, to the archbishop of Nicosia, written at the demand of Lawrence Urseti of Bergamo, vicar and inquisitor, concerning dues and payments owed by the Greek bishop of Soli to the archbishop of Nicosia. "Register," p. 491, no. 139. See also de Mas Latrie, *Histoire*, 3, pp. 538-39.

97. For an excellent treatment of the pact, as well as a listing and breakdown of each of the ten articles of this treaty, see D. Geanokoplos, *Emperor Michael Palaeologus* pp. 87-89. Article eight would have a bearing on the protection of Cypriote commercial interests by the Genoese fleet, which was now under direct Byzantine imperial orders.

98. LaMonte, "Register," p. 475, no. 93. Urban was anxious not only over the fate of Latin Greece proper, but also over the Greco-Genoese threat to the Latin held Greek islands, especially Negropont, Crete, and Cyprus. On January 12, 1263, he addressed a letter to the "bailli" and barons of Cyprus warning them against "insidious" designs of Michael to attack the island by plotting with the secular authorities.

99. LaMonte, "Register," p. 474, no. 95. De Mas Latrie, *Histoire*, 3, pp. 655-57; Potthast, mp/18476.

100. LaMonte, "Register," p. 476, no. 96. The pope threatened the bailli with excommunication if he did not assist the Latin archbishop against the Greeks, who were, along with the Latins themselves, allegedly practicing certain crimes, such as open adultery, sodomy, blasphemy, and games of chance; "Register," nos. 97 and 98; same date, to the archbishop.

101. For details of these treaties, see Setton, ed., *History of the Crusades*, 2, pp. 255-57.

102. The chief provisions of this cession were as follows:

1) Prince William of Achaia's daughter and heiress, Isabella, would marry Philip of Anjou, son of Charles.

2) William would retain the region of Achaia during his lifetime, subject to certain restrictions regarding donations and infeudations.

3) At the death of William, the principality would pass to Philip of Anjou or his children. Failing such successors, it would go to Charles himself. J. Longnon, "Le rattachement de la principauté de Morée au royaume de Sicilie en 1267," in *Journale de Savanta* (Paris, 1942), pp. 134ff. This work contains the whole treaty and an interesting analysis of it.

103. The introduction clearly states the objective: "Michael Palaeologos, the schismatic, having usurped the name of Emperor. . . has seized the imperial city of Constantinople and the whole Empire, expelled the Emperor Baldwin and the Latins residing there, and now only a part of the principality

of Achaea and Morea remains, of which he was also subjugated a considerable area. . . We, therefore, are ready with God's aid to undertake the pious task of restoring the noble limb severed by the schismatics from the body of our common mother, the Holy Roman Church." The treaty is printed in Del Giudice, 2, pp. 30ff. Geanakoplos, *Palaeologus*, p. 197, translated the above. The treaty provided also for the following: the Greeks and the Latins agreed to grant Venice all her former rights in the Latin Empire; they also agreed to assign all the islands, including Cyprus, except for Mytilene, Samos, Kos and Chios (which would remain in the possession of Baldwin and his heirs), to Charles who would be in full sovereignty. Del Giudice, 2, p. 37. Cf. Treaty of 1204, the "Partitio Romaniae," Tafel and Thomas, 1, pp. 476 ff.

104. The treaty is in Tafel and Thomas, 3, pp. 93-100. In essence this treaty admitted the Venetians to all parts of the Empire, including Cyprus, and exempted them from the payment of duties. In return, Venice promised not to ally with any power against "The Empire of Romania."

105. George Pachymeres, *De Michaele et Andronico Palaeologis*, ed. by I. Bekker, *Bizantina Historia*, ed. L. Schopen, I. Bekker (Bonn, 1830), 2, 123, pp. 3-8, 125: "Therefore, beset by so many difficulties which drove him to desperation, the emperor sends an envoy to the pope with the admonition to bring about the reconciliation and union of the churches of old and new Rome, with the understanding that the pope would avert the expedition of Charles." See also Michael's apprehensions of the Latins in these unionist attempts as mentioned by the Templar of Tyre in *Gestes des Chiprois in Recueil, Documents Arméniens*, 2 (Paris, 1906), p. 789.

106. Pachymeres, 2, 353, pp. 16-17. Gregoras, 2, 123, pp. 3-8.

107. Mansi, 24, col. 66. Cf. Hackett, p. 310, note 1: Papaioannou, 2, p. 75, note 1.

108. Pachymeres, 2, 386, pp. 12-13; 387, pp. 17-18.

109. LaMonte "Register," pp. 478-79, no. 102. See also Mansi, 26, cols. 318-19.

110. Mansi, 26, cols. 322-25. In this constitution, the Latins would be spiritual heads, while the Greeks would only be tolerated patiently. "Quare Latini episcopi sint in Cypri insula ordinati ipsi tolerati," col. 324.

111. LaMonte, "Register," p. 480, no. 104.

112. Hill, 3, p;. 1079.

113. The relationship between the emperor and the Church in the controversy of Caesaropapism among historians and theologians. Caesaropapism was the charge that the Byzantine Church was, in effect, a department of

the state resulting from the fact one person held both the religious and civil reigns of the empire. For the best treatment of this subject, see D. Geanakoplos, *Byzantine East and Latin West,* chap. 2, "The problem of Caesaropapism," pp. 55-83.

114. This tradition existed during the Arab raids from the middle of the eighth century to 965. The famous icon of Kykko allegedly goes back to the hand of Saint Luke and may be the one which the emperor in the eleventh century gave to the founder of the monastery.

CYPRUS AND CONSTANTINOPLE

1. De Mas Latrie, *Histoire,* 3, pp. 601-05; Hackett, pp. 479-80, note 2; Papaioannou, 3, p. 16, n. 20.

2. This document is found in Tafel and Thomas, 1, pp. 246-80. One can see the similarity between the plan to divide the empire in 1199, a similar plan devised for the island of Cyprus in 1196, and its actual occurrence in 1204 following the Fourth Crusade.

3. Geoffrey of Villehardouin, *The Conquest of Constantinople,* ed. and trans. N. de Wailly (Paris, 1874), pp. 59-60, 72-73. For details and commentary on the ramifications of the division, see Charles Diehl, "Fourth Crusade," *CMH,* p. 420. Also, see Donald M. Nicol in the more recent edition of *CMH* (1966), Chapter 7, "The Fourth Crusade and the Latin and Greek Empires, 1204-1261."

4. In addition to the abundance of literature written on the subject, the most recent bibliographies on the background of the Fourth Crusade and the diversion question include/ Robert de Clari, trans. Edgar Holmes McNeal, pp. 137-44; Geoffrey de Villehardouin, *La Conquete de Constantinople,* ed. Edmond Faral, (Paris, 1938-39), 1, lvi-lxvii; Hans Eberhard Mayer, *Bibliographie zur Geschichte der Kreuzzück* (Hanover, 1960) pp. 107-08; A. Frolow, *Recherches sur la Déviation de la IV Croisade vers Constantinople* (Paris, 1955), pp. 9-10; Edgar H. McNeal and Robert Lee Wolff, "The Fourth Crusade," in R. L. Wolff and H. W. Hazard, eds., *The Later Crusades: 1189-1311,* Vol. 2 of *A History of the Crusades,* ed. Kenneth M. Setton (Philadelphia, 1962), pp. 153-54, 169-71, notes 43-45, and other notes. For primary sources on the Crusade, see Brand, chap. 12, pp. 375-76, n. 1.

5. *The Devastatio Constantinopolitana* in *MGH, SS,* 16, also in *Chroniques Greco-romanes inédites ou peu connues,* ed. C. Hopf (Berlin, 1873), pp. 86-92, reveals that the pope sent delegates to Venice to procure a naval force great enough to transport the Crusaders east. Villehardouin, an envoy of Theobald of Champagne, says that the pope only gave him and

and the other envoys instructions to find a suitable seaport from which the expedition could be launched. They decided among themselves to go to Venice and negotiate with Dandolo, the Doge of Venice (Villehardouin, ed. Faral, chap. 14).

6. For this eyewitness account, see N. Choniates, pp. 854-68, *Historia Corpus Scriptorum Historial Byzantinae* (Bonn, 1835). Another eyewitness, Nicholas Mesarites, by this time metropolitan of Ephesos, confirms what Choniates says; Mesarites, "Oration," in *Neue Quellen Zur Geschichte des lateinischen Kaisertums und der Kirchenunion,* ed. A. Heisenberg (Munich, 1923), 1, pp. 41-48.

7. Villehardouin, chap. 250, p. 147.

8. In 1198 Pope Innocent III commissioned a priest, Fulk of Neuilly, to preach a crusade in and around Paris. One year later, at a tournament held in Champagne at Count Theobald's castle in Ecry, barons and nobles resolved to take up the cross and deliver the Holy Land. See Innocent III, *Epistolae,* 1, 398 (PL 204.378) and Ralph of Coggeshall, *Chronicon Anglicarum* (Rolls Series, 66), p. 130.

9. See the enlightening article by Palmer A. Throop, "Criticism of Papal Crusade Policy in Old French and Provencal" in *Speculum,* 13 (1930) 379-412. Throop points out that the first criticism of the pope for his neglect of the Holy Land at the expense of Constantinople and the East occurred in a Provencal *Sirvente,* composed by the troubadour Giraut de Bornehl (late twelfth century).

10. Choniates, pp. 226-48. See Brand, pp. 16-18, for an explanation of the importance of this defeat.

11. Choniates, pp. 325-26. See also John Danstrup, "Manual I's Coup against Genoa and Venice in the Light of Byzantine Commercial Policy," *Classica et Mediaevalia* 10 (1948) 195-219. For a discussion of the external and internal conditions of Venetian-Byzantine relations, see J. K. Fotheringham, "Genoa and the Fourth Crusade," *English Historical Review,* 25 (1910) 20-57, and A. F. Brown, "The Venetians and the Venetian Quarter in Constantinople to the Close of the Twelfth Century," *Journal of Hellenic Studies,* 40 (1920) 68-88.

12. See the definitive study of Geoffrey Barraclough, ed., *Eastern and Western Europe in the Middle Ages* (London, 1970), especially chapter 3 by Ferdinand Seibt, "The Religious Problems," pp. 83-124.

13. De Mas Latrie, *Histoire,* 3, p. 811.

14. *Histoire,* 3, pp. 813ff.

15. Histoire, 1, pp. 399-408; LaMonte, *Feudal Monarchy,* pp. 76ff.

16. See J. S. R. Boase, *Kingdoms and Strongholds of the Crusaders* (New York, 1971), pp. 166-70.

17. Gisleberti Chronicon Hanoniense, MGH SS., 21, p. 519. "First Latin Emperor of Constantinople," in *Speculum,* 27 (1952), pp. 281-83, and p. 303, n. 16.

18. Villehardouin, chap. 8, p. 6; Faral, 1, p. 10.

19. The originals survive in the archives at Mons; the charters, however, have been reprinted in journals. Wolff cites A. Wauters, *Table Chronologique des Chartes et diplômes imprimés concernant l' histoire de la Belgique,* 3 (Brussels, 1895). See Wolff, "Baldwin," n. 34.

20. "Baldwin" examines both of these codes. They are of interest because a similar pattern of governance was set up and at times abused during the early stages of the Latin empire in Constantinople following the Fourth Crusade; Wolff, "Baldwin," pp. 283-84.

21. According to Wolff in "Baldwin," who paraphrases a Monograph of Hainaut found in A. Pinchart, *Histoire du Conseil Souverain de Hainaut,* in *Memoires Couronées et autres memoires publiées par l' académie Royale des sciences, des lettres et des beaux arts de Belgique* (1858); a "bailli; gives justice to all persons and has jurisdiction in all cases as if he were the lord or count of Hainaut. The vassals of the lord or count must perform their duties fo justice for him as for the count or lord.

22. The Assizes de Romanie, written between 1303 and 1330, has its origins in the Latin Empire and from the customs established especially in the Morea (Peloponnesos). See G. Recoura, *Les Assizes de Romanie* (Paris, 1930), pp. 21ff. and 30ff., J. LaMonte's review of Recoura, *Speculum,* 7 (1932), 289-94; and "Three Questions Concerning the Assizes of Jerusalem," *Byzantinina-Meta-Byzantium,* 1 (1946) 201-11, especially pp. 208ff. See also P. W. Topping, "The Formation of the Assizes of Romania," *Byzantion,* 17 (1944-45) 304-19, in which he discusses the law codes and feudal institutions of Frankish Greece.

23. Gisleberti Chronicon Hanoniense, pp. 550-51.

24. Villehardouin, chap. 317, pp. 186-88; Faral, 2, p. 124.

25. Villehardouin, chap. 317, pp. 186-88; Faral, 2, p. 124.

26. Villehardouin, chap. 318, p. 186; Faral, 2, p. 126. See C. Du Cange, *Histoire de l' empire de Constantinople sous les empereurs français jusqu' à la conquête turque,* ed. J. A. Buchon (Paris, 1826), 1, p. 43, n. 3, who claims that she was buried in St. Sophia Cathedral.

27. Robert de Clari, p. 106: "... que on no sent onques que il deviut ... "

28. De Mas Latrie, *Chronique d' Ernoul,* p. 384: "... li Blac et li Comain. .. ocisent tous cens de le Compaignie l' empereur et lui avenc. ..."

29. Villehardouin, chaps. 439-41, pp. 262-64; Faral, 2, pp. 252-56. A letter by Henry confirming this and the fact that Baldwin died in prison are in Tafel and Thomas, 13, p. 37, no. 166. The letter relates the opposition of the Venetians to Henry's elevation and coronation.

30. The text of the treaty is in Tafel and Thomas, 1, pp. 464-88.

31. For a discussion of this book, see Miller, *The Latins in the Levant,* pp. 54-57. "Achaia" was part of the "Morea" (today's Peloponnesos). The emperor bestowed the title of "Prince of Achaia" on the masters of Morea. E.g., Innocent III conferred the title of "Prince of Achaia" on the first master of the Morea, William of Champlitte; after this, all princes were called "princes de la Moree"; see Setton, "The Latins in Greece," *CMH,* p. 391, n. 2.

32. See Peter W. Topping, *Feudal Institutions as Revealed in the Assizes of Romania,* University of Pennsylvania Translations and Reprints, third series (Philadelphia, 1949), for an authoritative discussion of the "assizes" and the light they throw on feudal institutions in Europe. A comparison of the "Partitio Romaniae" and the *Chronicle of Morea* reveals just how much of a pattern existed in the formation of Latin institutions in Greece and on Cyprus *per se.*

33. Chronicle of Morea, ed. J. Schmitt, 2, 2611-14. For the origin of the name "Morea," see Sir Rennell Rodd, *The Princes of Achaia and the Chronicles of the Morea, A Study of Greece in the Middle Ages* (London, 1907), his Appendix 1, pp. 270-72.

34. PL 225.699; Potthast, no. 2564, July 12, 1205.

35. PL 225.963; Potthast, no. 2860; in Tafel and Thomas 2, p. 19, no. 170.

36. See William Haumer, "The Concept of the New or Second Rome in the Middle Ages," *Speculum,* 19 (1944) 50-62, where the subject of "Roma Nova" and "Roma Secunda" are discussed.

37. This list is found in John Meyendorff, "St. Peter in Byzantine Theology," *St. Vladimir's Seminary Quarterly* 4 (1960) 34, who cites documents found in M. Jugie, *Theologia Dogmatica Christianorum Orientalium,* Vols. 1 and 4.

38. Meyendorff, says that Beveridge published this documnt for the first time in *Synodikon sive Pantectoe Canonum,* 2 (Oxford, 1672). F. Dvornik confirms that Photios could not be the author, *Photian Schism,* pp. 125-27,

138 Greeks and Latins on Cyprus

and *The Idea of Apostolicity in Byzantium and the Legend of the Apostle Andrew* (Cambridge, 1958), pp. 247-53.

39. These writings are published in *Sitzungsberichte der Bayrischen Akademie der Wissenschaften, Philos. Philolog. und Hist. Klasse,* and *Geschichte — Die Unionverhandlungen von 30 Aug. 1206,* 2; see Meyendorff, p. 47, n. 28 and 29.

40. Meyendorff, p. 47, note 30, refers to *Kriticheskie opyty po istorii drevnejshej greko-russkoj polemiki protiv Latinjan,* ed. A. Pavlov (St. Petersburg, 1878), pp. 158-68.

41. F. Dvornik, in *Apostolicity,* pp. 289-94, points out, however, that the argument is quite irrelevant for the Byzantines, in that the real problem lay in the concept of apostolicity itself, i.e., what constitutes a valid theory of "apostolic succession" and "infalliblility." Some Greek bishops obeyed Morosini. They rendered him the oath of fidelity and submission to the Apostolic See; see Wolff, "The Latin Patriarchate," pp. 33-60. See also PL 215.1030; Potthast, no. 2921, November 27, 1206. Wolff mentions Bishop Theodore of Negropont (Euboea), a Greek bishop who consented to obey Morosini and Innocent III. His superior was Berard, archbishop of Athens, who replaced the celebrated Michael Choniates, now in exile on the island of Chios. In 1208 Berard came into conflict with Theodore and complained to Innocent that Theodore did not want to be anointed according to the custom of the Latins. Theodore's anointment would have meant that his ordination in the Orthodox Church was invalid. Innocent intervened and commanded the archbishop of Neopatras, the bishop of Diavlia, and the abbot of the diocese of Negropont to restore Theodore to his throne; PL 215.1492; Potthast, no. 3552, December 8, 1208. This example showed the attitudes displayed by Innocent toward those Orthodox who went over to the Latins. See Magoulias, "Church Relations on Cyprus," pp. 75-106.

42. Miller, *Essays on the Latin Orient* (Cambridge, 1921), p. 177, says: "The Franks . . . simply annexed the existing Greek ecclesiastical organization . . . ousted the Orthodox hierarchy from their sees, and installd in their places Catholic ecclesiastics from the West." See Wolff, "The Latin Patriarchate," pp. 45-48 for numerous examples supporting this view. The pattern for this was set by the First Crusade. Crusader states of Antioch and Jerusalem had ousted Orthodox patriarchs. The papacy's formula for resolving the schism in the Greek East was to set Latin hierarchs over Greek subordinates.

43. Compare the lists of Latin "Provinciale" with the Greek lists, the "Notitiae Episcopatuum" or "Taxtiká" in Wolff's table (in "The Latin

Patriarchate''). One can reach the following conclusions:

1) The Greeks issued such lists for the purpose of defining the respective positions of the archbishops so that rankings at official functions would be observed.

2) These lists are important because they were revised at intervals during the Middle Ages and show the changes in rank of the various archdioceses.

44. Herakleia, for example, retained but six of the fifteen suffragans, over which it had jurisdiction under the Greeks but, in addition, received a former metropolitan and a former autocephalous archbishopric. Pegai, Chalcedon, Arkadiopolis, Nikomedia, Rhoussia, Apros, Ainos, Argos, Derkon, Messene, Lopadion, Kypsella, Maroneia, Aegina, Makre, Urosynopolis, Parion, Vrysis.

45. The sees of Athens, PL 215.1559; Potthast, no. 3654, February 13, 1209; Thessalonike, PL 216.555; Potthast, No. 4422, April 7, 1212; Philippi, PL 216.584; Potthast, no. 4472, May 22, 1212; and Corinth, PL 216.586; Potthast, no. 4478, May 22, 1212.

46. Of the ten Greek bishoprics subject to Athens, Innocent lists eight, the "Provinciale" four; of eleven subject to Thessalonike, Innocent lists six, the "Provinciale" only one.

47. In this respect the special register of Innocent III, *Regestrum Innocentii III Papae super negotio Romani imperii,* ed. Freidrich Kempf, in *Pontificia Universitate Gregoriana* (Rome, 1947), is a valuable document supporting this thesis. It is a compilation of the decisive correspondence during the crucial years of the contest of the German throne (1197-1209). Carefully planned and supervised by the pope, the register contains the bulk of the letters issued by the papal chancery as well as copies of the most important entries.

48. An excellent study of Innocent is found in *Innocent III: Vicar of Christ or Lord of the World?* ed. James M. Powell, in *Problems in European Civilization* (Boston, 1963).

49. Tafle and Thomas, 1, p. 502.

50. Innocent III, *Epistolae,* 7, 153, PL 215.455. In another letter Innocent wrote: ''Needless to say, although we are pleased to know that Constantinople has returned to obedience to its mother, the Holy Catholic Church, nevertheless we should be still more pleased if Jerusalem had been restored to the sovereignty of the Christian people,'' Letter 99, 139 and 957-58. Vasiliev's translation, p. 467.

51. Innocent III, *Epistolae*, 8, 133; PL 219.712 (Vasiliev's translation, p. 468.)

52. At the very moment of the Crusaders' triumphal entry into Constantinople after Alexios V Mourtzouphlos had already fled, Theodore Laskaris, son-in-law of Alexios III, crossed the straits to Asia Minor, persuaded the inhabitants of Nikaia to shelter his wife Anna and his three daughters, set up his capital at Brusa (Bursa), came to some kind of understanding with the Seljuks, and defeated three princelings who had set themselves up in the Malander valley. (See Runciman, *Crusades*, 3, pp. 122-23; Geanokoplos, *Emperor Michael Palaeologus*, pp. 14-15; Diehl, pp. 422-24.)

53. Stubbs, *Seventeen Lectures*, p. 193; N. Iorga, p.. 64. Stubbs makes this observation: "According to the *Assizes of Jerusalem*, every vassal who, whether immediately dependent on the king or on a mesne lord, had done homage to the king as chief lord, was a mmber of the royal court; a usage which in so small a state must have crushed out every tendency to representative government" (p. 194). As to *liege homage*, L. de Mas Latrie says: "All feudataries . . . are liegemen and do liege homage. Liege homage means that which they do, without respect or reservation of any other person, save the lord of Cyprus, neither to the emperor nor to any other; so it is ordained and declared by the Asizes. The barons used to grant fiefs and receive homage, but not the *ligece*, because the homage which was done of fealty to the barons was done with reservation of liege homage to the chief lord"; *Histoire*, 3, p. 532.

54. Emilianos, Κυπριακαὶ Σπουδαί, 1, pp. 200ff.

55. De Mas Latrie, *Histoire*, 2, p. 8. Turcopoles, members of the light cavalry, were trained as archers and were recruited from non-noble classes, mainly from the native population in countries occupied by the Crusaders. See L. Machaeras, 2, p. 77. *Recital Concerning the Sweet Land of Cyprus Entitled "Chronicle,"* 2 Vols. Greek text and English trans. R. M. Dawkins (Oxford, 1932).

56. See de Mas Latries, *Histoire*, 1, p. 44; also see LaMonte, *Feudal Monarchy*, p. 149. See Hill, 2, pp. 38ff.

57. In Machaeras, p. 26: "To some monthly payments, and to others rents and assignments, and judges to judge their cases . . . and to those of lower rank he granted freedom and liberties of enfranchisement." See also L. de Mas Latrie, *Histoire*, 1, p. 45.

58. De Mas Latrie, *Histoire*, p. 8; 3, p. 594. The Syrians seem to have had special privileges, paying only half the usual dues on sales and purchases.

59. Histoire, 2, p. 9, no. 1.

60. See L. de Mas Latrie, *Histoire*, 3, p. 614.

61. Details of this revolt are found in Hill, 2, pp. 36-38. See also de Mas Latrie, *Histoire*, 1, pp. 50ff.

CYPRUS AND LATIN THEOCRACY

1. A religious historian who died in the 1930s, Paul Alphandery saw the Crusades as an integral part of the medieval church, as he emphasized in the title of his great work, *La Chrétienté et l' idée de Croisade*, texte etabli par Alphonse Dupront, 2 vols. (Paris, 1954-59).

2. William L. Langer's presidential address of 1957 to the American Historical Association: "The Next Assignment," *American Historical Review* 63 (1958) 203-304, contains an interesting discussion of the values of the psychological approach to history.

3. The most recent book on the subject, which emphasizes this progressive scholarly debate through well-defined and meaningful stages, is Donald E. Queller's *The Latin Conquest of Constantinople* (New York, 1971).

4. PL 216.1025; F. Kempf, ed., p. 75. *Regestum Innocentii III Papae Super Negotio Romani Imperii. Miscellanea Historiae Pontificae.* (Rome, 1947). Cf. B. Tierney, *Foundations of the Conciliar Theory: The Contribution of the Medieval Canonists from Gratian to the Great Schism* (Cambridge, 1955). According to Tierney, the structure of the church in the thirteenth and fourteenth centuries was not a monolithic unity but rather a tense balance of conflicting forces; the contradictions between the definition of the church as a corporation of the faithful and the prevailing conception of papal sovereignty, which became apparent when the academic canonists discussed the status of the cardinals or the problem of a heretical pope or a schism. Tierney, apparently, excludes from his research the Latin East, where 'constitutional' elements in canonistic thought and principles of church government to preserve the faith and *status ecclesiae* overrode specific rights in specific contexts. In all fairness to Tierney's excellent book on the subject, this study certainly suggests one factor: the most fateful development in canon law in this period was not the development of the conflict between East and West, but the change from specific rights to a logically coherent system of church government in Rome, Cyprus, or Constantinople; this objective, by any stretch of the imagination, was totally improbable.

5. For an excellent summary of Eusebios' thought, which became a basis for Byzantine thinking on the subject, see N. Baynes, "Eusebius and the Christian Empire," in *Annuaire d' l' institut de philologie et d' histoire*

orientales, (1933-34), 2, pp. 13-18. C. F. Sherrard, *The Greek East and the Latin West. A Study in the Christian Tradition* (Oxford, 1959), pp. 92ff. See also F. Cranz, "Kingdom and Polity in Eusebius of Caesarea," *Harvard Theological Review,* 45 (1952) 47-66, and bibliography on p. 48. Also see the excellent study of Y. Congar, *After Nine Hundred Years* (New York, 1959), pp. 14-17.

6. W. Ullmann, *Medieval Papalism: The Political Theories of the Medieval Canonists* (London, 1949).

7. Watt, "The Language of Sovereignty," Part 2, *The Theory of Papal Monarchy in the Thirteenth Century* (New York, 1965), pp. 75-105.

8. LaMonte, *Feudal Monarchy,* p. 279.

9. This question is discussed at length in M. Wilks, *The Problem of Sovereignty in the Later Middle Ages* (Cambridge, 1963).

10. Letter of December 30, 1221, in Raynaldus, 1222, pp. 500-01. Potthast, no. 6747.

11. Letters of January 3, 1222. De Mas Latrie, *Histoire,* 2, p. 45; Potthast, no. 6755.

12. B. Tierney, "Papal Political Thought in the Thirteenth Century" *Medieval Studies,* 27 (1965) 245.

13. W. Miller, *Essays,* p. 78.

14. For a discussion of the oaths of obedience to be taken by the newly elected bishops, see Chapter 5. Also see Hill, 3, pp. 1059ff., and Hackett, pp. 114-23.

ORTHODOX AND LATINS: ECCLESIASTICAL DIFFERENCES

1. Every, *Byzantine Patriarchate,* pp. 152-94; Runciman, *Schism,* pp. 55-144.

2. Zernov, *Eastern Christendom* (London, 1963), pp. 101-08.

3. Zernov, pp. 90-91; Dvornik, *Byzantium and The Roman Primacy,* (New York, 1966), pp. 12-15.

4. The history of the *filioque* controversy has been the topic of many studies. For a comprehensive survey, see J. Gill, "Filioque," *New Catholic Encyclopedia* (New York, 1966), 5, pp. 913-14.

5. William Moore and Henry A. Wilson, "Select Writings and Letters of Gregory, Bishop of Nyssa," *Nicene and Post-Nicene Fathers,* ed. P. Schaff and H. Wace (Grand Rapids, 1954), 5, pp. 23-29. See also R. F. Harvanek,

"Gregory of Nyssa," *New Catholic Encyclopedia,* 4, pp. 794-96.

6. F. A. Sullivan, "Theodore of Mopsuestia," *New Catholic Encyclopedia* 14, pp. 18-19. Theodore of Kyrros (ca. 393-ca. 466) accused Saint Cyril of Alexandria (d. 444) of adhering to the innovation.

7. M. Hermanink, "Maximus Confessor," *New Catholic Encyclopedia,* 9, pp. 514-16. For a discussion in depth of the theological attributes of the Holy Spirit, see Vladimir Lossky, *The Mystical Theology of the Eastern Church* (London, 1957), pp. 62-65.

8. Zernov, pp. 90-91. His observation could very well be correct because the local Arians in Spain denied the equality of the Son to the Father. The statement that the Holy Spirit proceeded from the Father and the Son seemed to serve this purpose of stressing the equality of the Father and the Son. This precise wording helped them, so it would seem, to combat the Arianism of the Visigoths.

9. From Spain the *filioque* passed to the Carolingian court of Aix-la-Chapelle, where it found an eager advocate in Charlemagne. When Empress Irene of Byzantium broke the engagement of her son Constantine to Charlemagne's daughter Rotrud, he became determined more than ever to undermine the spiritual supremacy of Byzantium. He commissioned the scholars at his court to draw up the *Libri Carolini* (the Caroline Books) in an attempt to show that the Byzantine Church had succumbed to heresy by not accepting the *filioque,* among other things. See Anna Freeman, "Further Studies in the *Libri Carolini,* 7. The marginal notes in Vaticanus Latinus 7207" in *Speculum,* 46 (1971), pp. 597-612. Pope Leo III (795-816) wrote to Charlemagne diplomatically suggesting that although there was nothing theologically objectionable to the *filioque,* it would perhaps be a mistake to depart from the universally accepted version (see Magoulias, "Relations," pp. 97-99). Leo III, in fact, omitted the word when he ordered the Creed to be written on one section of the walls of Saint Peter's at Rome.

10. Photios, "Homily on The Annunciation," in Φωτίου Ὁμιλίαι, ed. Laourdas (Thessalonike, 1959), pp. 149ff.

11. See F. Dvornik, *Photian Schism: History and Legend* (Cambridge, 1948), pp. 383-402, where he draws a sketch of Greek traditional thinking and teaching on this subject until the twelfth century. The Roman Church, then in a state of decadence, did not officially adopt the *filioque* under the influence of the German Empire until the early eleventh century. After this a revitalized and militant Roman papacy made the issue a matter of dogma.

12. Cardinal Humbert, legate of Pope Leo IX in 1054, (PL 143.1003) to Gibbon, as to others, "reason, even of divines, might allow that the difference

is inevitable and harmless,'' Gibbon, *"History of the Decline and Fall of the Roman Empire,"* ed. J. B. Bury, 7 vols., 7th ed. (London, 1925), 6, p. 368. But the Greeks reasoned otherwise. The difference was, in fact, the expression of two opposing attitudes in religious thought. The Orthodox of the East with their apophatic practices preferred to avoid dogmatic definitions until the danger of heresy made them necessary. They would have been prepared to leave the question of the Holy Spirit unformulated. "You ask," said Gregory the Theologian, "what is the procession of the Holy Spirit. Tell me first what is the meaning of the Father not begotten, and I shall then explain to you the physiology of the generatin of the Son and the procession of the Spirit; and we shall both be stricken with madness for prying into the mystery of God," *Theologica Quinta; De Spiritu Sancto,* PG 36.141.

13. See the recent excellent book of Constance Head, *Justinian II of Byzantium* (Madison, 1971), in which she attempts to justify the much maligned Byzantine emperor.

14. Magoulias, "Relations," p. 92. For a reading of these canons, refer to Schaff and Wace, eds., *Nicene and Post-Nicene Fathers.*

15. Ibid.

16. The animosity between Greeks and Latins over *azyma* was seen in the martyrdom of thirteen Greek monks on Cyprus in 1231, when the Latin archbishop of Nicosia Eustorge ordered the Greeks to use *azyma* in their Holy Communion. When they refused, they were martyred.

17. See the informative work on eucharistic breads in the early Church by George Galavaris, *Bread and the Liturgy: The Symbolism of Early Christian and Byzantine Bread Stamps* (1970).

18. Bertram Colgrace, R. A. B. Mynous, eds., *Bede's Ecclesiastical History of the English People* (Oxford, 1969), pp. 78ff.

19. PG 220.836.

20. PL 143.744.

21. This work is in the edited study of A. Michel, *Humbert und Kerullarios,* 2 vols. (Paderborn, 1924-30), 2, pp. 322-42. For the events before, during, and after 1054, see D. M. Nicol, "Byzantium and the Papacy in the Eleventh Century," *The Journal of Ecclesiastical Studies,* 13 (1962) 1-20. See also Runciman, *The Eastern Schism: A Study of the Papacy and the Eastern Churches during the XIth and XIIth Centuries* (Oxford, 1955), pp. 28-54; Dvornik, *Byzantium,* pp. 124-53.

22. For a summary of the difference, see J. Gill, *The Council of Florence*

(Cambridge, 1961), pp. 270-304; Deno J. Geanokoplos, *Byzantine East and Latin West* (New York, 1966), pp. 84-109; F. Gavin, *Some Aspects of Contemporary Greek Thought* (London, 1936), pp. 129ff.; Henry C. Lea, *The History of Sacerdotol Celibacy in the Christian Church* (New York, 1957) pp. 61-70 and 143-307.

23. See Chrestos Androutsos, *Great Hereafter,* trans. William Roberts (Cleveland, 1956), for a rather precise position of the Eastern Orthodox Church on this difference with Rome.

24. The official Greek position may be found in Chrestos Androutsos [Symbolics from an Orthodox Viewpoint], 2nd ed. (Athens, 1930), pp. 357-58.

25. In 1205 Innocent III wrote to Baldwin, Latin emperor of Constantinople: "Since the Empire has passed from the Greeks to the Latins, it is mandatory to transform the rites which clerics perform; Ephraim has returned to Judah and should feed on the azymes of sincerity and truth, once old leaven has been disposed of"; PL 55.215, 623.

26. Hackett, p. 111.

27. "Fra Angelo Calepio, of Cyprus (of the Order of S. Dominic), to His Courteous and Kind Readers," in *Excerptia Cypria,* ed. and trans. Blaude Delaval Cobham (Cambridge, 1908), pp. 160-61.

28. See. W. B. Stevenson, *The Crusaders in the East* (Cambridge, 1907), pp. 347-55, for a detailed account of the last days of the Latin empire.

BYZANTINES AND LATINS: POLITICAL DIFFERENCES

1. See A. Schmemann, "The Idea of Primacy in Orthodox Ecclesiology," *St. Vladimir's Seminary Quarterly* 4 (1960) 49-75.

2. Gelasius, 1, *4, 2. Epistolae Romanorum Pontificum,* trans. Sister Agnes Bernard Cavanaugh in her dissertation, *Pope Gregory VII and the Theocratic State* (Washington, D.C., 1934), pp. 18-19.

3. For a discussion of the "Donation," see W. Ullmann, *A History of Political Thought: The Middle Ages* (London, 1965), pp. 58-66. In 751, Ravenna was captured by the Lombards. The exarchate of Ravenna had been the military and administrative center of the Byzantines, who were now powerless to offer any assistance to Rome. See Magoulias, pp. 93-94.

4. F. Grat, ed., *Annales de Saint-Bertin* (Paris, 1964), p. 107. Hincmar was the author of this account for the year 864. See W. Ullmann, *The Growth of Papal Government in the Middle Ages* (London, 1970), p. 208, n. 5, for additional references.

5. Einhardi Annales, Anno 794, *MGH* SS 181. See also W. Ullmann, *Growth of Papal Government,* p. 210.

6. For this position , see the definitive works of F. Dvornik, *Photian Schism,* and S. Runciman, *Schism.*

7. Runciman, *Schism,* p. 32.

8. Dvornik, *Photian Schism,* p. 253. Photios is referring to the teachings of the Byzantine Church concerning the *filioque* issue.

9. See Henry R. Percival, "The Seven Ecumenical Councils of the Undivided Church," Schaff and Wace, eds., p. 287. See excursus on Canon Twenty-eight, pp. 288-90. *MGH,* SS 3, *De Rebus Gestis Ottonis, Luitprand, Bp. of Cremona,* p. 345 and p. 25.

10. PL 142.1060ff.

11. Since a Roman pope is last mentioned in 1009, the omission would not seem to be mere coincidence. See Runciman, *Schism,* pp. 32-34.

12. See G. Every, *Byzantine Patriarchate* (London, 1962), 2nd rev. ed. pp. 149-50.

13. Cf. W. Ullmann, *Growth of Papal Government in the Middle Ages* (London, 1955), p. 267, n. 2.

14. G. Ostrogorsky, *A History of the Byzantine State,* trans. Joan Hussey (Oxford, 1956), p. 297.

15. A. Fortescue, *The Orthodox Church* (London, 1920), pp. 185-86. "To him (Humbert) the implementation of the primacy of the Roman Church was the cardinal point: the Roman Church is the hinge and head — 'cardo et caput' — of all the other churches." This principle "comprises also the Eastern half of Christendom." "The Western and Eastern Emperors are the arms of the pope." W. Ullmann, *Growth of Papal Government,* (see page 182) pp. 266, 267, 268.

16. R. Mayne, p. 142.

17. P. Charanis, "The Byzantine Empire," pp. 211-12. G. Ostrogorsky, p. 300 and references.

18. S. Runciman, *Schism,* pp. 56-57.

19. Gregory's policy is quite apparent in his letter to the Bishop of Chalon-sur Saone against Philip I. (*Registrum,* ed. E. Caspar, *MGH, Epistolae Selectae* (Berlin, 1920).

20. Joseph Strayer, *Feudalism* (Princeton, 1965), Anvil Original, No. 86, pp. 12-13. Cf. F. L. Ganshof, *Feudalism* (Harper Torchbooks), No. TB 1058, pp. 3-4.

21. Gregory VII, *Epistolae,* 147, col. 386. See subjective discussion of expedition in A. Cavanaugh, pp. 236-37.

22. P. Charanis, *Byzantine Empire,* pp. 188-89. In 1073 Michael VII addressed a letter to Gregory VII which was supplemented by an oral message related to the pope by those who brought the letter. Neither the letter nor a record of the oral message has survived, but a careful study of Gregory's reply and his various letters relating to the East indicate that the problem of the union of the churches and the need of the empire for military assistance to check the Turks constituted the subject matter of the imperial messages. See P. Charanis, "Byzantium, the West, and the Origin of the First Crusade," *Byzantion,* 19 (1949) 20ff.

23. On the subject of Turkoman power and occupation of the Holy Land, see C. Cahen, "La prèmiere Pénétration turque en Asie Mineure," *Byzantion,* 18 (1948) 5-67.

24. Frederick Duncalf, "The Pope's Plan for the First Crusade," *The Crusades and Other Historical Essays Presented to Dana C. Munro by his Former Students,* ed. L. J. Paetow (New York, 1920), pp. 44ff.

25. S. Runciman, *History of the Crusades,* 1, p. 99.

26. P. Charanis, "Byzantium, the West, and the Origin of the First Crusade," pp. 17-24. P. Charanis, "Byzantine Empire," 1, pp. 187-88. W. Ullmann, *Growth of Papal Government,* pp. 306-07. Cf. Einar Joranson, "The Inception of the Career of the Normans in Italy/ Legend and History," *Speculum,* 23 (1948) 353-97.

27. Gregory VII, *Epistolae,* 158, col. 388.

28. For an account of subjective anti-papal feelings, see Anna Komnene, *Alexiad, Collection Byzantine de l' Association Guillaume Budé,* ed. Bernard Leib, 3 vols. (Paris, 1937-45), 1, 13; English trans. E. R. A. Sewter, *The Alexiad of Anna Komnena* (Baltimore, Maryland, 1969), pp. 90-91.

29. Pertinent information concerning the improvement of East-West relationships at this time are found in August C. Krey, "Urban's Crusade, Success or Failure?" in *AHR,* 53 (1948), pp. 235-50; Bernard P. Leib, op cit., pp. 25-26, and *Les Patriarches de Byzance et la politique religieuse d' Aléxis I Comnéne 1081-1118),* in *Melanges Jules Lebretton,* II (Recherches de science religieuse), 40 (1952), pp. 201ff.

30. See W. Holtzmann, "Die Union zur Handlungen zwischen Alexios I und Papst Urban II," in *Byzantinische Zeitschrift,* 18 (1928) 38-67. G. Every, *Byzantine Patriarchate,* p. 177. Charanis, "Byzantine Empire," 1, p. 216.

31. P. Charanis, "Byzantine Empire," p. 217.

32. W. Holtzmann, pp. 42-43. Cf. Charanis, "Byzantine Empire," p. 218.

33. See Charanis, "Byzantine Empire," p. 218, and Frederick Duncalf, "The Councils of Piacenza and Clermont," in *A History of the Crusades,* ed. Setton, p. 227.

34. G. Ostrogorsky, pp. 318-19. D. C. Munro says: "The fact that Alexios had frequently asked for aid before the Council of Piacenza is universally admitted." "Did the Emperor Alexios I Ask for Aid at the Council of Piacenza?" in *AHR,* 27 (1922) 733, n. 11.

35. *Alexiad,* 8.5.1, p. 107.

36. James Bryce, *The Holy Roman Empire,* 3rd rev. ed. (New York, 1907), pp. 1, 89-120. Bryce's famous thesis is that medieval men were Christians only by virtue of their membership in the Church. Bertrand Russell agrees: "Throughout the Middle Ages, after the time of Charlemagne, the Church and the Holy Roman Empire were worldwide in idea, although everybody knew that they were not so in fact." B. Russell, *A History of Western Philosophy* (New York, 1945), p. 282. Ewart Lewis disagrees with both Russell and Bryce: "While the idea of universal empire certainly played a role in medieval speculations, that role was limited. It touched only certain minds, and few of those deeply. . . . Moreover, much of the loyalty which did focus on the concept of empire assumed an empire not necessarily defined in universal terms." E. Lewis, *Medieval Political Ideas,* 2 vols. (New York, 1954), 2, p. 430.

37. G. Barraclough, *History in a Changing World* (Oxford, 1956), pp. 38, 43, 45. Cf. Wallace K. Ferguson, *The Renaissance* (New York, 1940), pp. 13-19, especially p. 18, where he says: "One of the most significant results of the supremacy of the medieval Church was that it united the feudal society of western Europe in the common fellowship of Catholic Christendom . . . The Crusades were the military expression of this Christian unity."

38. One of the main chroniclers of the Council of Piacenza, as well as that of Clermont, was Bernold of St. Blaise, *Chronicon MGH* SS, 5, pp. 461-63.

39. Among the dignitaries present were Praxeda, the former queen of Henry IV, who went to Piacenza to accuse her husband of religious wrongdoings; representatives of King Philip of France, to argue against the excommunication imposed upon the king at the Council of Autun the previous year because he committed adultery; King Peter of Aragon, a vassal of the papacy, who agreed to pay an annual tribute. Bernold, p. 462.

40. Bernold, pp. 461-62. The "vow" had a long history as an ecclesiastical

institution. Ivo of Chartres and Gratian were the canonists who developed the concept of votive obligations. (Ivo's three canonistic collections — the *Decretum*, the *Panormia, and the Tripartita* — date from the years 1094-96, about the time of the Councils of Piacenza and Clermont. Gratian's famous work is the *Concordia Discordantium Canonum or Decretum*, which became the primary work for later studies in canon law.) For reference works, see Paul Fournier and Gabriel LeBras, *Histoire des Collections Canoniques en Occident depuis les fousses décrétals jusqu' au Décret de Gratien*, 2 vols. (Paris, 1931), 2, pp. 55-57, 105-06; Stephen Kuttnerr, *Harmony from Dissonance: An Interpretation of Medieval Canon Law* (Latrobe, Pa., 1960); James A. Brundage, "The Votive Obligations of Crusaders: The Development of a Canonistic Doctrine," *Traditio*, 24 (1968) 77-118.

41. See D. C. Munro, "The Speech of Pope Urban II at Clermont," *AHR*, 11 (1906) 231-42. For Urban's admonition against any abuses toward Christian brothers in the East, see F. Duncalf, "Councils," p. 242. Attitudes of Crusaders going to the East and development of the crusading movement are reviewed by L. C. MacKinney, "The People and Public Opinion in the Eleventh Century Peace Movement," *Speculum*, 5 (1930) 181-206; on the estrangement between Rome and Constantinople, see John Karmiris, "The Division of Christendom and Possibilities of Reunion," *The Greek Orthodox Theological Review* 2 (1955), pp. 160-75. The effects of this estrangement are discussed in Bernard Leib, *Rome, Kiev, et Byzance*, pp. 182-87; also in August C. Krey, *First Crusade: The Accounts of Eyewitness and Participants*. Reprinted, (Gloucester, 1958), pp. 235-50; Charanis, "Byzantine Empire," pp. 216-19; also by P. Charanis, "The First Crusade," pp. 19-36.

42. Alexiad, 2, p. 208, pp. 93-94. Albert of Aachen relates that, although Peter the Hermit's followers were destructive in the capital city, Alexios commanded that at no time were they to attack Crusaders because "they were Christians"; *Historia Hierosolymitana in Recueil des Historiens des Croisades: Historiens Occidentaux*, 5 vols. (Paris, 1844-1906); 4, pp. 282-89. See also S. Runciman, *Schism*, pp. 79, 85, 103-04; M. Villey, *La Croisade: l' état au moyen âge*, 6 (Paris, 1942), pp. 119-20.

43. Gibbon, 6, p. 287.

44. Raymond of Aguilers, *Historia Francorum qui ceperunt Iherusalem*, in *Receuil*, 7, p. 236.

45. Alexiad, 10.8, p. 324.

46. The development of papal imperialism is studied in John A. Watt, *The Theory of Papal Monarchy in the Thirteenth Century* (New York, 1965); see also Charles H. McIlwain, *The Growth of Political Thought in the West*

(New York, 1932), pp. 230-62, 276-88; R. W. and A. J. Carlyle, *A History of Medieval Political Theory in the West,* 6 vols. (Edinburgh and London, 1903-36), 5, pp. 152-440. Papal imperialism and its foundations have recently been developed by W. Ullmann, *The Growt of Papal Government.* For medieval conceptions of empire, see the study of Robert Folz, *L' Idée d' Empire en Occident du V au XIV siècle* (Paris, 1953).

47. Many of these contemporaries and historians and their works are analyzed by Giles Constable, "The Second Crusade as Seen by Contemporaries," *Traditio,* 9 (1953) 213-79. Runciman subjects the failures of the Crusade to thorough criticism, *Crusades,* 2, p. 288. A good balance and fair estimate appear in the account of Virginia Berry, "The Second Crusade," *A History of the Crusades,* ed. Setton, 1, pp. 465-66.

48. Saint Bernard, *De Consideratione,* trans. George Lewis (Oxford, 1908), p. 38, cited by Constable, p. 275.

49. V. Berry, pp. 486, 510-12; Runciman, *Crusades,* 2, pp. 266-67, 285-86.

50. Ferdinand Chalandon, in *Jean II Komnène (1118-1143) et Manuel Komnène (1143-1180)* (Paris, 1912), pp. 299-300, says that the French did not attack because rumors of German conquests in Asia Minor meant that there was nothing left for them to conquer. Berry, pp. 490-91, agrees with this view presenting Louis VII as friendly to Manuel, but emphasizing the influence that papal legates had upon crusaders in deterring their personal ambitions in favor of loyalty to papal crusade policy. Louis VII is given credit for avoiding a catastrophe at Constantinople by two French authorities: Louis Brehier, *Le Monde Byzantin: Vie et Mort de Byzance* (Paris, 1948), p. 330; and *L' Eglise et l' Orient au Moyen Age: Les Croisades,* 5th rev. ed. (Paris, 1928), p. 107. Also Rene Grousset, *Histoire des Croisades et du Royaume franc de Jerusalem,* 3 vols. (Paris, 1934-36), 2, pp. 238-39. Runciman seems to be unable to make up his mind. At one point he states that Louis' conscience and his satisfaction with Manuel who hosted him at Constantinople together with the wisdom of Bishop Arnulf of Lisieux worked together to save the city. Elsewhere, he gives all the credit to Arnulf who singlihanddly persuaded Louis not to attack the city despite the king's desire to do so. In both cases, Runciman assumes that the army wanted to take the city. See Runciman, *Crusades,* 2, p. 269; 3, p. 476; and Runciman, *Schism,* p. 126.

51. Odo de Deuil, *De Profectione Ludovici VII in Orientem,* ed. and trans. Virginia G. Berry, (New York, 1948), p. 12; see also Berry, p. 477.

52. Odo de Deuil, *De Profectione,* pp. 26-28; see also Berry, pp. 487-88; and Chalandon, *Jean II,* pp. 289-304. Earlier negotiations between Manuel

71. PL 214.112f. Basil, the metropolitan of Zagora, also sent his greetings to the pope, and a "prince" named Bellota wrote as king asking that he and his family be admitted to the Church of Rome, PL 214.1115-16.

72. For a detailed discussion of the letter and its far-reaching implications, see Wolff's article, pp. 168-90.

73. PL 214.1113. A detailed account of the papal relations with the Bulgarian Empire up to A.D. 1018 is found in Runciman, *A History of the First Bulgarian Empire* (London, 1930), chap. 3, pp. 99ff.

74. PL 214.1116, 1118.

75. Theiner, 1, 29, no. 46, in Wolff: p. 196. Wolff reflects on a series of letters sent by Innocent in 1204. The pope decided to send Ioannitsa a cardinal: "Karissimo filio in Christo Caloiohanni illustri Bulgarerum et Blachorum regi" in exchange for which he was to sweat loyalty to Rome. Basil, also, was to be his primate (Wolff). See also PL 215.277.

76. PL 215.428. On November 15, the legate left Tirnovo taking with him two boys, the son of a priest named Constantine and the son of Ioannitsa, to study Latin in Rome.

77. Robert de Clari, *La Conquête de Constantinople,* ed. P. Lavar (Paris, 1924), pp. 63-65; trans. Edgar H. McNeal (New York, 1936), pp. 86-88. Villehardouin mentioned nothing of this embassy, perhaps because, as a leading policy-maker in the crusade, he may have been partly responsible in accepting aid from Ioannitsa. Niketas Choniates, however, was aware of this embassy. When Ioannitsa sent ambassadors to discuss diplomatic relations with the Latin host, they asked him to address them, not as a king would address his friends, but as a lowly slave would address his lord and master. The implication is that, if this subservient relationship did not exist, the Crusaders would invade his lands and reduce him to his former position. For this reason, Choniates related, Ioannitsa welcomed certain Greek nobles, who were former officers of Alexios III whom Boniface of Montferrat and Emperor Baldwin had dismissed. Choniates, *Historia,* pp. 808-09.

78. See H. Pissard, *La Guerre sainte en pays Chreétien* (Paris, 1912), pp. 122-25.

79. See Palmer A. Throop, *Criticism of the Crusade,* Nu. Swers and Zeiteinger (Amsterdam, 1940), p. 48, n. 102, who says that after John of England had taken the cross, Innocent III made this declaration in favor of John in his excommunication of rebellious barons: "Pejores procul dubio Saracenis existentes, cum illum conantur a regno depellere, de quo potius sperabatur, quod deberet succurrere terrae Sanctae"; Roger de Wendover, *Flores Historiarum,* 2, 152.

80. See Palmer A. Throop, *Criticism of the Crusade,* Nu. Swers and Zeiteinger (Amsterdam, 1940), p. 48, note 102, who says that after John of England had taken the cross, Innocent III made this declaration in favor of John in his excommunication of rebellious barons: "Pejores procul dubio Saracenis existentes, cum illum conantur a regno depellero, de quo potius sperabatur, quod deberet succurror terrae Sanctae" (Roger de Wendover, *Flores Historiarum,* 2, 152.

81. Pissard, pp. 121-42.

82. The eloquent work of William Miller, *The Latins in the Levant* (New York, 1968), bears witness to this fact. With the establishment of the Latin Empire of Constantinople, the Greeks fled to Asia Minor and there, at Nikaia, the city of the First Ecumenical Council in A.D. 325 and at Trebizond on the shores of the Black Sea, fonded two empires, of which "the former served as a basis for the reconquest of Byzantium, while the latter survived for a few years the Turkish conquest of the new Rome"; see p. 1.

83. Under the government of the La Roche family, the duchy of Athens lasted until 1311. After the battle of the Kephisos, the duchy passed to the Catalans, (1311-34) who were superseded by the Florentine family of Acciajuoli (1334-56). The Byzantines never again regained possession. The principality of Achaia, governed by three Villehardouins (1204-70), also remained in foreign hands for centuries. For information on the Latin sovereignty in Greece from 1204 to 1566, see W. Miller, especially "Table of Frankish Rulers," pp. 651-54.

84. When Innocent III again sought to promote a crusade in 1213, his attempts caused a tumult throughout Europe. In France especially there was a storm of discontent at the arbitrary procedure of the papal legate, who infringed upon the feudal rights of nobles and royalty. Eudes III of Burgundy complained to Philip Augustus that the pope had no right to substitute his ecclesiastical jurisdiction for the feudal in the interest of a crusade. Philip Augustus seized this opportunity to draw up a list of grievances against the legate to suspend or change ordinary legislation while the crusade was being preached. This entire issue is discussed by Achille Luchaire, *Innocent III: La Question d' orient* (Paris, 1907), pp. 286-91. See also Luchaire, *Social France in the Reign of Philip Augustus,* for other contributing factors: e.g., Philip's "marriage" problems in Flanders, trouble with England, troublesome vassals, etc.

85. Even those who took the cross at this time showed themselves recalcitrant. "They have the cross on their clothes but not in their heart," wrote Innocent (PL 216.729).

86. Upon the outbreak of the Welsh War, Edward I seized all the tithe money deposited in churches and monasteries on March 28, 1283. After the war ended, Edward restored the money. However, he eventually acquired it again after bargaining with the pope. See W. E. Lunt, "Papal Taxation in England in the Reign of Edward I," *English Historical Review,* 30 (1915) 410, 411, 416.

87. In a letter to Leo X, who preached a crusade against the Turks in 1517, Frances I of France declared plainly that the people had been deceived so often in holy wars, especially since the days when the Fourth Crusade had been diverted from the Holy Lands to Constantinople, that there was little hope of their supporting it financially or otherwise. See C. Kohler's review of E. Bourlaton's article, "La Croisade prochée dans le diocèse de Maillezais, de Mars 1517 a Juillet 1518," *Revue du bas-Poitou,* 8 (1895) 353-71, found in *Revue de d' Orient latin,* 8 (1901) 575.

88. A related point is made by Throop, p. 289: "The decay of the crusading movement indicated by the criticism offered during the pontificate of Gregory X convinces one that the real crisis of the papal monarchy came before the dramatic debacle of Boniface VIII. Contemporary objections to the crusade prove that the papacy had lost one of its most powerful weapons against the rising national state."

15. View of the left ear of the d' Avila bastion

Glossary

Archaiomanteis — Greek colonists from Achaia who brought with them to Cyprus priests or seers known as "archaiomanteis."

Archikynegos — Captain of the royal hunt; also a title of the "strategos."

Azyma — The Latin usage of unleavened instead of leavened bread in Holy Communion.

Ballistae — A military engine resembling a bow, stretched with cords and thongs used to hurl stones or other missiles; used extensively in Cypriote warfare.

Basileus — This title, used interchangeably with "autokrator," refers to the emperor. On Cyprus he was also the governor-general, having the title of "strategos" of the island.

Basse Cour — Otherwise known as "the Court of Bourgeois" on Cyprus, organized under viscounts (sheriffs) and acting as courts of law on a local level. (See contrasting *Haute Cour.*)

Byzant (or *Bezant*) — Gold coin used in Byzantium and current throughout the then known world.

Caesar — Title ranking below the "sebastokrator" (see below); reserved usually for the imperial family or granted to outsiders for important services to the state.

Caesaropapism — The absolute control over all aspects of the Church, even in matters of dogma, which are usually reserved for the discretion of ecclesiastical authority.

157

Casales — Community groups on Cyprus.

Cataphract — A soldier armed from head to foot, sometimes riding a horse similarly protected.

Charistikon — A method, developed by Alexios Komnenos, by which monastic property was handed over to the care of a private person.

Christotokos — Refers to Mary, who gave birth to Christ, not God (in contrast to "Theotokos").

Chrysobull — Also called *Golden Bull*, an imperial decree, written in purple ink, with a golden seal.

Consularis — A pronvicial governor on Cyprus, who was appointed by the governor of the diocese, or by the emperor on his recommendation.

Curoplates — One of the three highest honors, with "Caesar" and "Noblissimus," and normally conferred only on members of the imperial family.

Despot — Highest ranking official after the emperor. The title sometimes implied a limited kind of sovereignty or even right of succession to the throne and was usually granted to relatives within the realm, but on rare occasions to foreigners.

Drungarios — Commander of a "drungus," a body of infantry, whom one might equate with a modern battalion commander.

Druzhina — A corps of soldiers, usually applied to the famous Varangians who formed the emperor's personal bodyguard.

Enzyma — The leavened bread used by the Greek Church in the sacrament of Holy Eucharist.

Eparch — The Greek equivalent of the Roman "praefectus" (one in charge, a governor or commander). The "eparch" was "father of the city," the most important civil official in Constantinople after the emperor himself. On Cyprus he was also a revenue official.

Epiklesis — The Litany of the Holy Spirit which changes the bread and wine into the Body and Blood of Christ.

Epistemonarches — Originally meant one who is in charge of the sciences. In Byzantium he was the official responsible for the proper clerical administration of the hierarchy.

Excubitae — Mounted troops normally stationed in Constantinople and commanded by a Domestiko (an ecclesiastical official ranking immediately after the two heads of the antiphonal choirs in Hagia Sophia of Constantinople).

Filioque — The Latin innovation to the Nicaean Creed of the First and Second Ecumenical Synods. With this innovation the Latin Creed read: ". . . and the Holy Spirit. . . which proceedeth from the Father *and the Son*."

Grammateus — An adjutant-general or quarter-master general of the military forces on Cyprus.

Grand Constable — Commander of the Latin mercenaries in the Byzantine Empire, ranking next to the "Protostrator," and the "Grand Stratopedarch." The title was in imitation of the Norman Constable.

Grand Domestic — Commander-in-chief of the imperial army; high-ranking title generally reserved for close relatives to the emperor.

Grand Logothete — Highest ranking minister of the Empire.

Grand Primikerios — One of the officers of the imperial household. The dignity was reserved for eunuchs. Master of ceremonies in the imperial palace.

Grand Stratopedarch — High official in charge of armaments and provisions for the troops.

Haute Cour — The governing royal court of thirteenth-century Cyprus made up of all the barons of the island. Included in this group were nobles and clergy who had fiefs and certain holdings.

Hegemonies — Separate regiments of Cyprus had their own commanders with this title. (In the case of the cavarly, they were known as "hipparchai.") They were all under the "Grammateus."

Helepolis — A wooden tower moved oln rollers or wheels and used to assault enemy wails in sieges.

Homoiousion — The term meaning that Christ, the second Person of the Holy Trinity, is of similar essence or substance with the Father, the first Person of the Holy Trinity.

Homoousion — The term meaning that Christ, the second Person of the Holy Trinity, is the very same essence or substance with the Father, the first Person of the Holy Trinity.

Hypatos — From the eighth century, he governed the island as imperial legate. The "Katapan" replaced him in the eleventh century.

Hypostasis — A term denoting the essence of the triune Godhead.

Indiction — Originally, the term was used in reference to an announcement of a levy of foodstuffs to be delivered to the imperial government. From A.D. 312 it was used as a chronological term. From A.D. 537 all documents had to be dated by the indiction number which corresponded to a cycle of fifteen years and which was related to other systems of dating.

Katapan — From the eleventh century the imperial legate of Cyprus who governed the island with full sovereign powers.

Limenarcha — Governor of the inspector of the harbors of Cyprus, although probably not an imperial official.

Magistros — A high court official. The title was conferred on many persons, each with his own sphere of action, but like many others its importance gradually declined. On Cyprus he was "master of the imperial household."

Mathesep — A Cypriote official assisting the "viscount" or local sheriff. The whole derives from the Arabic "Muhtasif," or inspector of weights and measures.

Megas Dukas — Literally, a grand duke and admiral of the imperial fleet, most of the time only nominally in command.

Megas Kyr — Literally, great lord, a title by which the Burgudian Duke of Athens-Thebes was known to his Greek subjects. The Lusignans were sometimes referred to by this title.

Metousiosis — A term denoting the process of chang of the bread and wine into the Holy Eucharist during the Divine Liturgy.

Mnemosynon — Memorial prayers for the deceased in the Eastern Orthodox ritual.

Monophysite — One who believes that Christ had only one nature, the divine, which absorbed the human. The heresy was condemned by the Fourth Ecumenical Council (A.D. 431).

Monothelite — One who maintains that Christ had two natures, human and divine, united in one Person, but with only one will. The heresy was condemned by the Sixth Ecumenical Council (A.D. 680-81).

Nomophylax — "Guardian of the law." The head of the Legal Faculty at the University of Constantinople.

Obol — A small Greek coin, equivalent to a farthing, a sou, or a cent.

Orphanotrophos — The supervisor of the orphanages, usually in the capital cities of each Eparch.

Parakoimomenos — Literally, "one who sleeps near (the emperor)." The Lord Chamberlain who was an eunuch also performed other duties of state.

Peltast A light-armed soldier with a round target shield.

Phangoumes — A general name for leading Cypriote families of noble lineage.

Poitarides — Travelling troubadors on Cyprus who sang "Akritic" ballads from Asia Minor and cast them in their own idiom. While this class of ballad-singers had disappeared elsewhere, on Cyprus it has survived to the present day.

Polychroneia — Byzantine musical acclamations which were addressed to a newly enthroned emperor.

Praefectus Praetorio Orientis — Under Diocletian and then Constantine the Great, the Empire was reorganized into dioceses. Cyprus fell into the first of the twelve great dioceses, commanded originally by the "perfectus praetorio Orientis" literally meaning "the commander in command of the East."

Primikerios — An official in the palace.

Proedros — A high senatorial dignitary.

Prokathemenos tou Vestiariou — Minister of finance who had replaced the "Logothete of the Treasury."

Proskynesis — The physical act of prostration before emperor or icon. Also, the act of venerating an icon or God.

Protokynegos — Court official who held the imperial stirrup while the emperor or king mounted. He was also in charge of the hunt.

Protopresbyteros — The highest title (honorary) that is bestowed upon a cleric who is married.

Protospatharios — The Commander of the "spatharii" or "sword-bearers," who formed part of the imperial bodyguard.

Protostrator — Commander of the vanguard and light-cavalry troops.

Protovestiarites — An official originally connected with the imperial chamber. In Byzantine times, he was connected with the military command.

Protovestiarios — The officer in charge of the imperial wardrobe and the monies used to purchase the wardrobe. At times he ranked higher than the "Grand Domestic."

Quaestor Justinianus exercitus — In A.D. 735 Justinian reformed the provincial organization of the Empire by which five provinces (Scythia, Moesia, Caria, all the islands of Cyclades and Cyprus) were grouped together under the command of the above official.

Romania — The name given to the Latin empire of Constantinople and the name used by the Latin emperors as part of their titles on their seals and in their correspondence. Originally, it meant the territory of the Empire in the East.

Romphalia — A one-edged heavy sword of iron.

Satrap — Originally, a Persian title. Satraps governed provinces. The Turks took over the title but used it more widely and efficiently. In essence, a satrap was a local governor.

Sebastokrator — A high official making just below the "Despot." The title was reserved for members of the imperial family.

Secreta — These were the officers used by various civil authorities in connection with the finances of the department of treasury. These officers were closely associated to the "Logothete."

Stade — A Greek measurement, approximately the equivalence of a furlong.

Stater — A Greek coin, of gold or silver, of a fixed weight.

Stauropegion — A Community of monks or nuns which acquires priviledges allowing it to become free from local control and subject only to the patriarch.

Strategat — A military district.

Strategos — The General or commander, who was governor of a province of "theme" of the Empire.

Stratia — A tax, also called the "hearth-tax" (kapnikon), directed especially to Cypriote villagers. It amounts to three *hyperpers* (gold besants), or six aspers (silver besants) for each village hearth.

Tagmatarch — The brigadier in charge of a brigade, whose strength was estimated roughly at 3000

Tatars of the Court — Tutors of the heir-apparent to the throne.

Themes — Originally, this meant army corps and afterwards came to be applied to the district or province occupied by an army corps and governed by a "strategos." (The "themes" were divided into "tunmai" governed by officers bearing the title of "turmarchs," while the turma was again subdivided into lieutenancies [topoteresiai] and "banda," which were similarly administered by soldiers, "drungarii" and counts.

Theotokos — In reference to Mary, who gave birth to God incarnate.

Vestiarios — Title of honor, in this period usually connected with the administration of the treasury. Originally, it meant one of the officials under the "protovestiarios."

Zeon — Warm water mixed with the wine in the chalice prior to the blessing which changes the elements into Holy Communion.

Bibliography

A. Primary Sources, Collections (General) and Encyclopediae

Acta Sanctorum. Begun at Antwerp in 1643 and Venice in 1730. Paris ed. 61 vols. 1863-83.

Amadi, Francesco. *Chroniques d' Amadi et de Strambaldi. Collection de documents inédits sur l' histoire de France.* Ed. Louis de Mas Latrie. Paris, 1891.

Berger, E. *Les Registres d' Innocent IV.* Vol. 1. Paris, 1884.

Bustron, Florio. *Cronica. Collection de documents inedits sur l' histoire de France.* L. de Mas Latrie. Paris, 1888.

Cheney, C.R., and Cheney, Mary G. *The Letters of Pope Innocent III (1198-1216).* Oxford, 1967.

Gams, Pius Bonifacius. *Series Episcoporum Ecclesiae Catholicae.* Grax, 1957.

Gappuyns, N. *Le Synodikon de Chypre au XIII Siecle.* Vol. 2, no. 10. Paris, 1935.

Germon, L. de, and Polain, L. *Catalogue de la bibliothèque de feu M. Le Comte Riant.* 2 vols. Paris, 1899.

Herbermann, C. G., and others, eds. *The Catholic Encyclopedia.* 12 vols. New York, 1951ff.

Hill, Rosalind, ed. *Descriptio sanctorum locorum Hierusalem. Gesta Francorum et aliorum Hierosolymitanorum: The Deeds of the Franks and the Other Pilgrims to Jerusalem.* "Medieval Texts." Ed. V. H. Galbraith *and others.* London, Edinburgh, Paris, Melbourne, Toronto, and New York, 1962.

Hopf, Charles. *Chroniques greco-romaines inédites ou peu Connues.* Berlin, 1873.

Jaffé, Philipp, and Löwenfeld, Samuel, eds. *Regesta Pontificum Romanorum.* 2nd ed. 2 vols. Leipzig, 1885-88.

LaMonte, John. "A Register of the Cartulary of the Cathedral of Santa Sophia of Nicosia." *Byzantion,* 5 1929-30), pp. 373-482

Mansi, G.C. *Sacrorum Conciliorum Nova et Amplissima Collectio.* 53 vols. Florence, Venice, 1759-1798.

Mas Latrie, L. de, ed. *Chroniques d' Ernoul et de Bernard le Trésovier.* Paris, 1871.

Mas Latrie, L. de, ed. *Documents genois concernant l' île de Chypre.* Paris, 1894. Also, *Archives de L' Orient Latin.* Vol. 2, pt. 2, pp. 170-76.

Mas Latrie, L. de, ed. "Documents nouveaux servant de preuves à l' histoire de l' île de Chypre sous le regne des princes de la maison de Lusignan." *Collection de documents inédits sur l' histoire de France.* Paris, 1882.

Mas Latrie, L. de, ed. "Nouvelles preuves de l' histoire de Chypre." *Bibliothèque de l' Ecole des Chartes.* Vols. 32 and 34. 1871.

Paetow, A.C. *Guide to the Study of Medieval History.* Rev. ed. New York, 1931.

Palestine Pilgrims Text Society Library. Committee of the Palestine Exploration Fund. 13 vols. London, 1890-97.

Percival, Henry. "The Seven Ecumenical Councils of the Undivided Church." *Nicene and Post-Nicene Fathers of the Christian Church.* Vol. 14. Michigan, 1956.

Potthast, August. *Bibliotheca Historica Medii Aevi (375-1500 A.D.).* 2 vols. Berlin, 1896.

Potthast, August. *Regesta Pontificum Romanorum.* 2 vols. Berlin, 1874-1875.

Raynaud, G., ed. *Les Gestes des Chiprois; Recueil de Chroniques françoises écrites en orient aux XIIIᵉ et XIVᵉ siècles.* (Philippe de Novare et Gérard de Monvéal.) Société de l' orient latin. Geneva, 1887. Also, *Recueil de historiens des Croisades. Document Arméniens.* Vol. 2.

Recueil des historiens des Croisades. Academie des inscriptions et belles-lettres. Paris, 1841-1906. A. *Historiens Occidentaux.* 5 vols.

1841-95. B. *Lois (Assizes de Jérusalem)*. 2 vols. 1841-43. C. *Historiens Orientaux*. 5 vols. 1872-1906. D. *Historiens Grecs*. 2 vols. 1875-81. E. *Documents Arméniens*. 2 vols. 1869-1906.

Rerum Britannicarum medii aevi scriptores. (Chronicles and Memorials of Great Britain and Ireland during the Middle Ages.) London, 1858-1911. (Rolls Series). 99 vols. London, 1858-96. *Sources and Literature of English History from the Earliest Times to about 1485*. Rev. 2nd ed. New York, 1915.

Rian, Comte, ed. *Archives de L' Orient Latin*. Publiées sous le patronage de la Societé de l' Orient Latin. 2 vols. Paris, 1881-84.

Rian, Comte, ed. *Exuviae Sacrae Constantinopolitanae*. Fasciculus documentorum minorum, ad byzantina lipsana in Occidentem saeculo XIII; translata, spectantium ad historiam quarti belli sacri imperii gallo-graeci illustrantium. 3 vols. 1877-1904.

Röhricht, R. *Regestra regni hierosolymitani (MXCVII-MCCXCI)*. Vol. 1 *Peni Ponti*. Nos. 658ff. *Haymar Monachi. De expugnata A.D. MXCXI Accone liber tetrasticus*. P. Riant. Paris, 1885.

Tafel, G.L.F., and Thomas, G.M. *Urkunden zur altern Handels — und Staatsgeschichte der Republik Venedig, Fontes Rerum Austriacarum, Diplomata et Acta, XII-XIV*. Vienna, 1856-57.

B. Primary Sources and Collections (Greek)

Acropolita, George. *Annales. Corpus Scriptorum Historiae Byzantinae*. Bonn, 1836.

Chalcocondyles, L. *Historiarum de origine ac rebus gestis Turcarum*. (Greek text and Latin translation.) PG 159. French translation by Blaise de Vigenaire. *Histoire de 1208 a 1483*. 2 vols. Paris, 1662. Also, *Laonici Chalcocondylae Historiarum Demonstrationes*. Ed. E. Davico. Vol. 2. Budapest, 1927.

Choniates, Nicetas. *Historia. Corpus Scriptorum Historiae Byzantinae*. Bonn, 1835.

Comnena, Anna. *Alexiad. Collection byzantine de l' Association Guillaume Budé*. Ed. Bernard Leib. 3 vols. Paris, 1937-45.

Corpus Scriptorum Historiae Byzantinae. Bonn, 1828-97.

Cotelerius, J.B. *Criminationes Adversus Ecclesiam Latinam*.

Monumenta Ecclesiae Graecae. Vol. 3. Paris, 1677-92.

Darrouzès, J., ed. "Les documents byzantines du XIIe siècle sur la primautè romaine." *Revue des études byzantines.* 23 (1965) 42-88.

Darrouzes, J., ed. *Documents inédits d' ecclésiologie byzantine.* Paris, 1966.

Εὐστάθιος, Ἐπίσκοπος Θεσσαλονίκης. *Προσφώνησις Ἰσαὰκ Ἀγγέλου.* Eustathii Metropolitae Thessalonicensis Opuscula. (Tafel and Thomas, eds.) Frankfort, 1852.

George of Cyprus. Laudatio Michaelis Palaeologi. PG, 142. 346-86. Also, *Anecdota Graeca.* Ed. J. Boissonade. Vol. 1. Paris, 1829.

Gregoras, Nicephoras. *Historia Byzantina (1204-1477).* Corpus Scriptorum Historiae Byzantinae. Ed. I. Bekker. 2 vols. Bonn, 1829-35. Also, PG 148.

Grumel, V. *Les Regestes des actes du patriarcat de Constantinople. Les Actes des Patriarches.* Vol. 1. Fasc. 1, 381-715; Fasc. 2, 715-1043; Fasc. 3, 1043-1206. Thouars, France, 1932, 1936, 1947, in progress.

Koukoules, Phaedo, ed. *Θεσσαλονίκης Εὐσταθίου τὰ Λαογραφικά.* 2 vols. Athens, 1950.

Lambros, Spyridon P., ed. *Μιχαὴλ Ἀκομινάτου τοῦ Χωνιάτου τὰ σωζόμενα.* 2 vols. Athens, 1879-80.

Laourdas, Basil. "The Letter of Photios to the Archbishop of Aquileia: Two Notes on its Texts." *Κληρονομία* (1971) 66-68.

Laourdas, B. ed. "Φωτίου Πατριάρχου Κωνσταντινουπόλεως: Ὁμιλία ἐπὶ τοῦ Εὐαγγελισμοῦ." *Φωτίου Ὁμιλίαι.* Thessalonike, 1959.

Leo of Ochrid. *Epistola ad Ioannem Episcopum Tranensem.* PG 120. 836.

Mesarites, Nicholas. *Λόγος ἀφηγηματικός. Nikolaos Mesarites: Die Palastrevolution des Joannes Konemenos.* Wurzburg, 1907.

Pachymeres, George. *De Michaele Paleologe, De Andronico Paleologo. Corpus Scriptorum Historiae Byzantinae.* Bonn, 1835. Also, PG, Vols. 143-44.

Phrantzes, George. *Annales (1259-1477). Corpus Scriptorum Historiae Byzantinae.* Bonn, 1838. Also, *PG,* Vol. 116.

Ράλλης, Φ. καί Ποτλῆς, Μ. *Σύνταγμα τῶν ἱερῶν κανόνων.* 6 vols. Athens, 1852-69.

Sathas, C. Άσίζαι τοῦ βασιλείου τῶν Ἱεροσολύμων καὶ τῆς Κύπρου. *Bibliotecha Graeca Medii Aevi*, 6. Paris, 1877.

Sathas, C. Μνημεῖα Ἑλληνικῆς Ἱστορίας. *Documents inédits relatifs à l' histoire de la Grèece.* 9 Vols. Paris, 1880-90.

Schmitt, John, ed. Τὸ Χρονικὸν τοῦ Μορέως (The Chronicle of Morea). London, 1904.

C. Primary Sources and Collections (Latin)

Acta Romanorum Pontificum a S. Clemente (an. c. 90) ad Coelestinum III (m. 1198). Pontificia Commissio ad redigendum Codicem iuris Canonici Orientalis. 2 vols. Vatican, 1943.

Auvray, L., ed. *Les Registres de Gregoire IX.* 4 vols. 1896-1955.

Bacon, Roger. *Opus Majus.* Ed. J.H. Bridges, III. Oxford, 1960.

Benedict of Peterborough. *Gesta regis Henrici secundi Benedicti abbatis. Rolls Series.* Vol. 1.

Delisle, Leopold. "Lettres inédites d' Innocent III." *Bibliothèque de l' école des Chartres.* Vol. 34. 1873, pp. 397-419.

Ernoul. *Chronique d' Ernoul et de Bernard le Trésorier.* Ed. Edmond Faral. 2 vols. Paris, 1938-39.

Gisleberti Chronicon Hanoniense. MGH. SS. Vol. 21.

Gratian. Decretum. Friedberg. *Corpus Iuris Canonici.* Vol. 1.

Gregory IX. *Decretalium Collectiones.* Friedberg. *Corpus Iuris Canonici.* Vol. 2.

Gunther of Paris. *Historia Constantinopolitana.* Riant. *Exuviae Sacrae Constantinopolitanae.* Vol. 1.

Hopf, Carl. *Chronista Novgorodensis. Chroniques greco-romaines. Pp. 93-98.* (Translated into Latin).

Hopf, C. *Devastatio Constantinopolitana. Chroniques greco-romaines inédites ou peu connues.* Pp. 86-92.

Humbert of Silva Candida, Cardinal. *Adversus Graecorum Calumnias (Dialogus inter Romanum et Constantinopolitanum).* Leo IX. *Epistolae. PL* 143.

Innocent III, Pope. *Acta Innocentii (1198-1216).* Ed. P.T. Haluscynskyj. *Pontificia Commissio . . . iuris Canonici Orientalis*, Fontes. 3 ser. Vol. 2. Vatican, 1944.

Innocent III, Pope. *Appendix ad Regesta. PL* 216.

Innocent III, Pope. *De Sacro Altario Mysterio. PL* 117.

Innocent III, Pope. *Epistola.* Batiffol.

Innocent III, Pope. *Epistolae.* Holtzmann.

Innocent III, Pope. *Epistolae. PL* 214 and 217.

Innocent III, Pope. *Epistolae.* Tafel and Thomas. Vols. 12, 13.

Innocent III, Pope. "Lettres inédites d' Innocent III." *Bibliothèque de l' école de Chartres.* Ed. Leopold Delisle. Vol. 314. 1873. Pp. 397-419.

Innocent III, Pope. *Regestum Innocentii III Papae Super Negotio Romani Imperii.* Ed. Friedrich Kempf. Rome, 1947.

Ivo of Chartres. *Decretum. PL* 141.

Kempf, F., ed. *Regestum Innocentii III Papae Super Negotio Romani Imperii. Miscellanea Historiae Pontificae.* Rome, 1947.

Migne, J.P. *Patrologiae Cursus Completus, series latina.* 221 vols. Paris, 1844-55. Index, 4 vols. Paris, 1862-64.

Muratori, L.A., ed. *Rerum Italicarum Scriptoras (1672-1751).* 25 Vols. Vol. 2. Milan, 1723-51.

Paris, Matthew. *Chronica Majora.* Ed. H. Luard. *Rolls Series.* Vols. 2, 5. London, 1874.

Pertz, G.H., Mommsen, T., and others, eds. *Monumenta Germaniae Historica.* Reichsinstitut für ältere deutsche Geschichtskunde. Hanover, 1826 and ff.

A. Alberic of Trois Fontanies. *Chronicon. MGH. SS.* Vol. 23. *Recueil des historiens des Gaules et de la France.* Vol. 18. Paris, 1758-1904.

B. *Annales Colonienses Maximi. MGH. SS.* Vol. 17.

C. Anonymous of Halbrstadt. *De Peregrinatione in Greciam. MGH. SS.* Vol. 23. Riant, *Exuviae Sacrae Constantinopolitanae.* Vol. 1.

D. Ansbert. *Expeditio Friderici Imperatoris. Quellen zur Geschichte des Kreuzzugs Kaisers Friedrich I.* Ed. Anton Chroust. *MGH. SS. New Series. Berlin, 1928.*

E. Gregory VII. *Das Register Gregors VII.* Ed. Erich Caspar. *MGH. Epistolae Selectae.* Vol. 2. pt. 1. Berlin, 1955.

F. *Monumenta Germaniae Historica . . . Scriptores Rerum Germanicarum.* New Series, 10 vols. 1922 and ff.

Pressutti, I., ed. *I regesti del Pontefice Onorio III.* Rome, 1884.

Pressutti, I., ed. *Regesta Honorii Papae III.* 2 vols. Rome, 1880-95.
Ralph of Coggeshall. *Chronicon Anglicarum. Rolls Series.* Vol. 66.
Theiner, August. *Vetera Monumenta Slavorum meridionalium
historiam sacram illustrantia.* Vol. 1. Rome, 1863.

D. Modern and Secondary Works in Greek

Άγαθαγγέλου, Μητροπολίτου Κυδωνίας καὶ Ἀποκορώνου.
"Περὶ τῆς θέσεως τοῦ Ἑλληνικοῦ κλήρου ἐπὶ Βενετοκρατίας,"
Ἐκκλησιαστικὸς Φάρος, (1937) 512-18.
Άδαμαντίου, Ἀδ. "Τὰ Χρονικὰ τοῦ Μορέως," *Δελτίον Ἱστο-
ρικῆς καὶ Ἐθνολογικῆς Ἑταιρείας τῆς Ἑλλάδος,* 10 (1906) 453, ff.
Αἰμιλιανίδου, Ἀχιλλέως. "Προνόμια τῶν ἀλλοδαπῶν καὶ
διομολογήσεις ἐν Κύπρῳ," *Κυπριακαὶ Σπουδαί,* 1 (1937) 1-59.
Ἀνωνύμου. " Ἡ Ἐκκλησία τῆς Κύπρου, ἱστορικὴ ἐπισκόπη-
σις," Ὁ Ἀπόστολος Βαρνάβας, 9 (1948) 129-40.
Βαγενᾶ Θ. *Χρονικὰ τῆς Κύπρου, ἀγῶνες τῶν Κυπρίων γιὰ τὴν
ἐλευθερία.* Athens, 1956.
Γενναδίου, Μητροπολίτου Ἡλιουπόλεως. *Ἱστορία τοῦ Οἰκουμε-
νικοῦ Πατριαρχείου.* Athens, 1952.
Γενναδίου. "Τοῦ Οἰκουμενικοῦ Πατριάρχου Ἀθανασίου Α΄
Ἐπιστολομιαῖαι διδασκαλίαι πρὸς τὸν Αὐτοκράτορα Ἀνδρόνικον
Β΄," *Ὀρθοδοξία,* 27 (1952) 12-15.
Δένδιας, Μιχαὴλ Α. " Ἐπὶ μίας ἐπιστολῆς τοῦ Φρειδερίκου Β΄
πρὸς Ἰωάννην Δούκαν Βατάζην," *Ἐπετηρὶς Ἑταιρείας Βυζαντινῶν
Σπουδῶν,* 13 (1937) 400-11.
Διονυσιάτου, Εὐθυμίου μοναχοῦ. "Περὶ τοῦ ἐν Τραπεζοῦντος
ἐμφυλίου πολέμου τινά. Χρυσόβουλλον Ἀλεξίου Γ΄ Κομνηνοῦ,
αὐτοκράτορος Τραπεζοῦντος, *Ποντιακὴ Ἑστία,* 6 (1955) 342-43.
Διομήδη, Ἀλέξανδρου Ν. " Ἡ ἐξέλιξις τῆς φορολογίας τῆς γῆς
εἰς τὸ Βυζάντιον," *Ἐπετηρὶς Ἑταιρείας Βυζαντινῶν Σπουδῶν,* 19
(1949) 306-14.
Δοανίδου, Σοφία Ἰ. *Αἱ μητροπόλεις καὶ ἀρχιεπισκοπαὶ τοῦ Οἰκουμενικοῦ Πατριαρχείου καὶ ἡ τάξις αὐτῶν.* Athens, 1934.
Δυοβουνιώτης, Κ. "Νεοφύτου Ἐγκλείστου ἀνέκδοτα ἔργα,"
Ἐπετηρὶς Ἑταιρείας Βυζαντινῶν Σπουδῶν, 13 (1937) 40-49.

Έταιρείας Κυπριακῶν Σπουδῶν. "Οἱ "Αγιοι Καρπασίας, Φίλων, Συνέσιος, Θύρβος, Φωτεινή, Σωζόμενος. Εἰσαγωγὴ καὶ κείμενον ἀκολουθιῶν καὶ συναξαρίων ἐπὶ τῇ βάσει τοῦ χειρογράφου Ἀκακίου μοναχοῦ τοῦ Κυπρίου μετ' εἰκόνων," *Κυπριακαὶ Σπουδαί*, 11 (1948) 112. ff.

Ζακυθηνός, Διονύσιος Α. "Μελέται περὶ τῆς διοικητικῆς διαιρέσεως καὶ τῆς ἐπαρχιακῆς διοικήσεως ἐν τῷ Βυζαντινῷ κράτει." *Ἐπετηρὶς Ἐταιρείας Βυζαντινῶν Σπουδῶν*, 17 (1941) 208-74; 18 (1948) 42-62; 19 (1949) 3-25; 21 (1951) 179-209; 22 (1952) 159-82; 25 (1955) 127-57.

Ζέππος, Παναγιώτης. "Τὸ δίκαιον εἰς τὰς Ἑλληνικὰς Ἀσσίζας τῆς Κύπρου," *Ἐπετηρὶς Ἐταιρείας Βυζαντινῶν Σπουδῶν*, 25 (1955) 306-30.

Ζέππος, Π. "Τὸ δίκαιον εἰς τὸ Χρονικὸν τοῦ Μορέως," *Ἐπετηρὶς Ἐταιρείας Βυζαντινῶν Σπουδῶν*, 18 (1948) 202-20. Θεοχαρίδου, Γ. "Οἱ Σταυροφόροι ἄρχοντες τῆς Μητροπόλεως Θεσσαλονίκης, *Μακεδονικά*, 3 (1948) 379-81.

Καρατζᾶ, Κ.Ν. " Ἀσσίζαι τῶν Ἱεροσολύμων καὶ τῆς Κύπρου," *Νέα Σιών*, 10 (1907) 897.

Καργώτου, Γ. "Δύο χειρόγραφα τῆς ἐν Κύπρῳ ἱερᾶς Μονῆς τῆς Παναγίας τοῦ Μαχαιρᾶ," *Κυπριακαὶ Σπουδαί*, 15 (1952) 42-78.

Κεραμόπουλος, Α. Δ. *Τί εἶναι οἱ Κουτσόβλαχοι*. Athens, 1939.

Κληρίδου, Ν. "Κυπριακὴ ἁγιογραφία. Προλεγόμενα καὶ κείμενον τῆς ἀκολουθίας τοῦ ὁσίου καὶ θεοφόρου πατρὸς ἡμῶν Ἰωνᾶ τοῦ θαυματουργοῦ, τοῦ ἐν Περγάμῳ τῷ χωρίῳ," *Κυπριακαὶ Σπουδαί*, 1 (1937) 89-132.

Κληρίδου, Ν. *Μοναστήρια στὴν Κύπρο. Θρύλοι καὶ παραδόσεις*. Leukosia, 1952.

Κόλια, Γεωργίου Τ. " Ἡ ἐξωτερικὴ πολιτικὴ Ἀλεξίου Α΄. Κομνηνοῦ, 1081-1118," *Ἀθηνᾶ*, 59 (1955) 241-88.

Κονιδάρη, Γ. Ἰ. *Αἱ μητροπόλεις καὶ ἀρχιεπισκοπαὶ τοῦ Οἰκουμενικοῦ Πατριαρχείου καὶ ἡ τάξις αὐτῶν*. Athens, 1934.

Κονιδάρη, Γ.Ἰ. " Ἡ Θέσις τῆς Αὐτοκεφάλου Ἐκκλησίας τῆς Κύπρου ἔναντι τοῦ Οἰκουμενικοῦ Πατριαρχείου κατὰ τὸν Θ΄. καί Ι΄. αἰῶνα," *Πρακτικὰ τῆς Ἀκαδημίας Ἀθηνῶν*, 18 (1943) 135-46.

Κουγκέα, Σ. " Ὁ Γεώργιος Ἀκροπολίτης κτήτωρ τοῦ Παρισινοῦ κώδικος τοῦ Σουίδα," *Byzantina-Metabyzantina*, 1,2 (1949) 61-74.

Κουκουλέ, Φαίδων Ί. ''Αἱ ὁδοὶ καὶ ἔμβολοι τῶν Βυζαντινῶν πόλεων,'' *Ἐπετηρὶς Ἑταιρείας Βυζαντινῶν Σπουδῶν*, 18 (1948) 3-26.

Κουκουλέ, Φ.Ι. *Βυζαντινῶν βίος καὶ πολιτισμός*. Vol. 3. Athens, 1949.

Κυριαζῆ, Ν. '' Ἡ Κύπρος ὑπὸ τοὺς Λουζινιανούς,'' *Κυπριακὰ Χρονικά*. Κύπρος, (1937) 55 ff.

Κυριαζῆ, Ν. '' Ἐκ τῶν κωδίκων τῆς Μητροπόλεως Κιτίου,'' *Κυπριακὰ Χρονικά*, (1937) 81-144.

Λαμψίδη, Ὀδ. ''Τινὰ περὶ ἀνωνύμων λιβέλλων ἐν Βυζαντίῳ,'' *Ἐπετηρὶς Ἑταιρείας Βυζαντινῶν Σπουδῶν*, 18 (1946) 144-52.

Μπόνη, Κωνσταντίνου Γ. '' Ὁ Θεσσαλονίκης Εὐστάθιος καὶ οἱ δύο τόμοι τοῦ Αὐτοκράτορος Μανουὴλ Α.΄ Κομνηνοῦ, 1143-1180, ὑπὲρ τῶν εἰς τὴν Χριστιανικὴν Ὀρθοδοξίαν μεθισταμένων Μωαμεθανῶν,'' *Ἐπετηρὶς Ἑταιρείας Βυζαντινῶν Σπουδῶν* 19 (1949) 162-69.

Μέρτζιου, Κ. Δ. '' Ὁ Φραγκῖσκος Μοροζίνι, ἡ Κασσάνδρα, ἡ Καβάλλα καὶ ἡ Θάσος. Αἱ διενεργηθεῖσαι κατ᾽ αὐτῶν ἐπιδρομαί,'' *Μακεδονικά*, 3 (1955) 1-7.

Πάλλη, Α. '' Ἡ Φραγκοκρατία στὴν Ἑλλάδα,'' *Κυπριακὰ Γράμματα*, 13 (1948) 63-72.

Πάλλη, Α. ''Τὸ Χρονικὸν τοῦ Λεοντίου Μαχαιρᾶ,'' *Κυπριακὰ Γράμματα*, 13 (1948) 355-65.

Παναγίδη, Ἀμφιαράου. *Συγχρονισμοὶ τῆς Ἑλληνικῆς καὶ Κυπριακῆς πρὸς τὴν παγκόσμιον ἱστορίαν*. Cyprus, 1948.

Παπαδοπούλου, Χρυσοστόμου. *Τὸ πρωτεῖον τοῦ ἐπισκόπου Ρώμης*. Athens, 1964.

Παπαρρηγοπούλου, Κωνσταντίνου. *Ἱστορία τοῦ Ἑλληνικοῦ Ἔθνους*. Vol. 4. Athens, 1925.

Παπαχαραλάμπους, Γ. '' Ἔθιμα, προλήψεις, καὶ δεισιδαιμονίαι τῶν Κυπρίων,'' *Κυπριακαὶ Σπουδαί*, 1 (1937) 89-132.

Πασχάλη, Δημ. '' Ἡ Δυτικὴ Ἐκκλησία εἰς τὰς Κυκλάδας ἐπὶ Φραγκοκρατίας,'' *Ἀνδριακὰ Χρονικά*, 2-3 (1948) 5-136.

Πασχαλίδου, Ἀγγελικῆς. ''Τύποι καὶ συνθέσεις ἀπὸ κυπριακὲς τοιχογραφίες τοῦ 15ου καὶ 16ου αἰῶνα,'' *Κυπριακαὶ Σπουδαί*, 12 (1949) 1-25.

Πιλαβάκη, Κ. ''Γλωσσικαὶ παρατηρήσεις εἰς Jean Darrouzès: Un

174   Greeks and Latins on Cyprus

Obituaire Chypriote, Le Parisinus Graecus 1588," Κυπριακὰ Γράμματα, 17 (1952) 338-52.

Ρωμανίδου, Ἰωάννου Πρωτοπρ. "Οἱ Ἅγιοι Κύριλλος καὶ Μεθόδιος. Ἕλληνες ἀντιπρόσωποι Λατίνων εἰς Σλαύους ἔναντι Φράγκων," Ὀρθόδοξος Τύπος, 153 (January,1972) 155; (February 1972).

Σήφακα, Γ. "Τὸ Χρυσόβουλλον Ἀλεξίου Β΄ Κομνηνοῦ καὶ τὰ δώδεκα ἀρχοντόπουλλα," Κρητικὰ Χρονικά, 2 (1948) 129-40.

Σιάτου, Α. Μία ποινικὴ δίκη κατὰ Μιχαὴλ Παλαιολόγου, μὲ θεοκρισίαν. Athens, 1938.

Σπυριδάκη, Κ. Σύντομος Ἱστορία τῆς Κύπρου. Leukosia, 1964.

Στεφανίδου, Β. Ἐκκλησιαστικὴ Ἱστορία. Athens, 1948.

Σωτηρίου, Γ. Α. " Ὁ Ναὸς καὶ ὁ τάφος τοῦ Ἀποστόλου Βαρνάβα παρὰ τὴν Σαλαμῖνα τῆς Κύπρου," Κυπριακὰ Χρονικά, 1 (1937) 175-87.

Σωτηρίου, Γ.Α. Τὰ Βυζαντινὰ μνήματα τῆς Κύπρου. Vol. 1. Athens, 1935.

Χαριτωνίδου, Χ. Παρατηρήσεις κριτικαὶ καὶ γραμματικαὶ εἰς Ἄνναν Κομνηνήν. Athens, 1951.

Χατζηψάλτη, Κ. "Συμβολαὶ εἰς τὴν ἱστορίαν τῆς Ἐκκλησίας τῆς Κύπρου κατὰ τὴν Βυζαντινὴν περίοδον," Κυπριακαὶ Σπουδαί, 18 (1956) 27-45.

Χατζηψάλτη, Κ. "Σχέσεις τῆς Κύπρου πρὸς τὸ ἐν Νικαίᾳ Βυζαντινὸν κράτος. Αἱ περὶ τῆς Ἐκκλησίας Κύπρου δύο πρὸς Ἰωάννην Βατάτζην ἐπιστολαὶ τοῦ Ἑρρίκου Α΄ Λουζινιὰν καὶ τοῦ Ἀρχιεπισκόπου Νεοφύτου," Κυπριακαὶ Σπουδαί, 15 (1952) 65-82.

Χριστοφίδου, Μύρωνος. "Τὰ ἐπώνυμα τῆς Παναγίας ἐν Κύπρῳ," Κυπριακὰ Γράμματα, 14 (1949) 92-94.

Χρυσάνθη, Κύπρου. "Εὐθύνες καὶ ποινὲς ἰατρῶν κατὰ τὶς Ἀσίζες," Κυπριακαὶ Σπουδαί, 12 (1949) 175-84.

Χρυσανθοπούλου, Ε. "Νέαι πηγαὶ τοῦ Χρονικοῦ τῆς Μονεμβασίας," Πρακτικὰ Ἀκαδημίας Ἀθηνῶν, 26 (1952) 166-71.

Τσικνοπούλου, Ἰωάννου Π. "Κίνητρα καὶ πηγαὶ τοῦ συγγραφικοῦ ἔργου τοῦ ἐγκλείστου Ἁγίου Νεοφύτου, Κυπριακαὶ Σπουδαί, 18 (1955) 73-92.

E. Secondary Works

Alexander, Paul J. "A Chrysobull of the Emperor Andronicus II Palaeologus in Favor of the See of Kanina in Albania, *Byzantion,* 15 (1940-1941) 167-207.

Alphandery, P. *La Chrétienté et l' idée des Croisades.* Paris, 1954.

Andrea, Alfred J. *Pope Innocent III as Crusader and Canonist: His Relations with the Greeks of Constantinople, 1198-1216* (Dissertation). Cornell University, 1969.

Archer, T.A. *The Crusade of Richard I (1189-1192).* London, 1900.

Atiya, A.S. *Crusade, Commerce and Culture.* Bloomington, IN, 1962.

Atiya, A.S. *The Crusade in the Later Middle Ages.* London, 1930.

Atiya, A.S. "The Crusades: Old Ideas and New Conceptions." *Journal of World History,* 2 (1954-55) 469-75.

Attwater, D. *The Christian Churches of the East.* 2 vols. Milwaukee, Wisconsin, 1947-49.

Baldwin, Marshall W. "The Papacy and the Levant during the Twelfth Century." *Bulletin of the Polish Institute of Arts and Sciences in America,* 3 (1945) 277-87.

Bladwin, Marshall W. "Some Recent Interpretations of Pope Urban's Eastern Policy." *Catholic Historical Review,* 25 (1940) 459-66.

Bellamy, C.V., and Jukes-Browne, A.J. *The Geology of Cyprus.* Plymouth, 1905.

Boase, T.S.R. *Kingdoms and Strongholds of the Crusaders.* Indianapolis and New York, 1971.

Bon, A. "Recherches sur la principauté d' Achaie 1205-1430." *Etudes Medievales offertes à A. Fliche.* Paris, 1952, 7-21.

Bramhill, E. "The Privileges of the Crusaders." *American Journal of Theology,* 5 (1902) 279 ff.

Brand, Charles M. "The Byzantines and Saladin, 1185-1192: Opponents of the Third Crusade." *Speculum,* 37 (1962) 167-81.

Brand, Charles M. *Byzantium Confronts the West, 1180-1204.* Cambridge, Massachusetts, 1968.

Brehier, Louis. *L' Eglise et l' Orient au moyen âge: Les Croisades.* 6th ed. Paris, 1928.

Brehier, Louis. *Les institutions de l' empire byzantin.* Paris, 1949.

Brehier, Louis. *Le monde byzantin.* 3 vols. Paris, 1947.

Brehier, Louis. *La Querelle des images.* Paris, 1904.

Brehier, Louis. *Le Schisme oriental du XIe siècle.* Paris, 1899.

Brown, Elizabeth A.R. "The Cristercians in the Latin Empire of Constantinople and Greece, 1204-1276." *Traditio,* 14 (1950) 63-120.

Brown, Horatio F. *Studies in the History of Venice.* Vol. 2. London, 1907.

Brown, Horatio F. "The Venetians and the Venetian Quarter in Constantinople to the Close of the Twelfth Century," *Journal of Hellenic Studies,* 40 (1930) 68-88.

Brundage, James A. "The Crusade of Richard I: Two Canonical *Quaestiones,*" *Speculum,* 38 (1963) 289-310.

Brundage, James A. "The Crusades, Motives and Achievements." *Problems in European Civlization.* Boston, 1964.

Brundage, James A. *Medieval Canon Law and the Crusader.* Madison, Wisconsin, 1969.

Brundage, James A. "A Note on the Attestation of Crusaders' Vows," *Catholic Historical Review,* 52 (1966) 234-39.

Brundage, James A. "Recent Crusade Historiography: Some Observations and Suggestions," *Catholic Historical Review,* 49 (1964) 493-507.

Brundage, James A. "The Votive Obligations of Crusaders: The Development of a Canonistic Doctrine," *Traditio,* 24 (1960) 77-118.

Bryce, James. *The Holy Roman Empire.* 3rd. rev. ed. New York, 1907.

Buchon, J. *Recherches historiques sur la principauté française de Morée et les hautes baronnies.* 2 vols. Paris, 1845.

Bury, J.B. "The Fall of Constantinople." *Yale Review.* N.S. 3 (1913-1914) 56-77.

Cambridge Medieval History. Vol. 4. Ed. by J.B. Bury. New York, 1923.

A. Diehl, C. "The Fourth Crusade and the Latin Empire." *CMH.* Vol. 4. 1923. Reprinted, 1936, pp. 415-31.

B. Miller, William. "The Empire of Nicaea and the Recovery of Constantinople," *CMH.* Vol. 4. 1923, pp. 478-516.

C. Nicol, D.M. "The Fourth Crusade and the Greek and Latin Empires, 1204-1261." *CMH.* Vol. 4. 1923. Pt. 2, pp. 275-330.

Cambridge Medieval History. Vol. 4. Parts 1 and 2, Ed. J. M. Hussey. Cambridge, 1966, 1967.

Cannon, Lillian R. *History of Christianity in the Middle Ages.* New York, 1960.

Carlyle, A.J. and R.W. *A History of Mediaeval Political Theory in the West.* 6 vols. Edinburgh and London, 1903-36.

Cavanaugh, Sister Agnes Bernard. *Pope Gregory VII and the Theocratic State* (Dissertation). Catholic University of America, 1934.

Chalandon, Ferdinand. *Essai sur le règne d' Aléxis I Comnène (1081-1118).* Paris, 1900.

Chalandon, Ferdinand. *Histoire de la Première Croisade jusqu à l' élection de Godefroi de Bouillon.* Paris, 1925.

Chalandon, Ferdinand. *Jean II Comnène (1118-1143) et Manuel I Comnène (1143-1180).* 2 vols. Paris, 1912. Reprinted, New York; 1960.

Charanis, Peter. "Aims of the Medieval Crusades and How They Were Viewed by Byzantium," *Church History,* 16 (1952).

Charanis, Peter. "The Aristocracy of Byzantium in the Thirteenth Century," *Studies in Roman Economic and Social History for A. C Johnson.* Ed. R. Coleman-Norton. Princeton, 1951, pp. 336-55.

Charanis, Peter. "On the Social Structure and Economic Organization of the Byzantine Empire in the Thirteenth Century and Later" *Byzantinoslavica,* 12 (1951) 94-153.

Clement, Oliver. *L' Essor du Christianisme Oriental.* Paris, 1964.

Cobham, D.D. *An Attempt at a Biliography of Cyprus.* Nicosia, 1929.

Cobham, D.D. *Excerpta Cypria, Material for a History of Cyprus.* Cambridge, 1908.

Congar, Yves. *After Nine Hundred Years.* New York, 1959.

Constable, Giles. "The Second Crusade as Seen by Contemporaries," *Traditio,* 9 (1935) 213-80.

Constantelos, Demetrios. *Byzantine Philanthropy and Social Welfare.* New Brunswick, 1968.

Cranz, F. "Kingdom and Polity in Eusebius of Caesarea," *Harvard Theological Review,* No. 45. 1952, pp. 47-66.

Creighton, M. *A History of the Papacy from the Great Schism to the Sack of Rome.* 6 vols. London, 1897.

Cullis, C.A. "Sketch of the Geology and Mineral Resources of

Cyprus," *Journal of Social Arts*. New York, 1924, 624-47.

Curtis, Edmund. *Roger of Sicily and the Normans in Lower Italy, 1016-1154*. New York and London, 1912.

Daly, William M. "Christian Fraternity, the Crusaders, and the Security of Cosntantinople, 1097-1204: The Precarious Survival of an Ideal," *Mediaeval Studies*, 22 (1960) 43-91.

Daskalakis, A. P. *L' hellenicité de Chypre et le droit d' un peuple de disposer librement de ses destiniees. Reponse aux arguments anglais*. Cyprus, 1952.

Delaville, LeRoulx J. *Les Hospitaliers en terre Sainte et a Chypre, 1100-1310*. Paris, 1904.

Diehl, C. "Les Monuments de l' Orient Latin," *Rev. Or. Lat.*, 5 (1897) 293-310.

Diehl, C. "The Byzantine Empire and the Crusades," *Essays on the Crusades*. Burlington, Vermont, 1903, pp. 91-118.

Dikigoropoulos, A.I. "The Church of Cyprus during the Period of the Arab Wars, A.D. 649-965," *The Greek Orthodox Theological Review*, 11 (1965-66) 237-79.

DuCange, C. *Histoire de l' Empire de Constantinople sous les empereurs français*. 1st ed. Paris, 1657. New ed. by J.S. Buchon. 2 vols. Paris, 1826.

Dvornik, Francis. *Byzantium and the Roman Primacy*. New York, 1966.

Dvornik, Francis. "L' encyclique de Photius aux Orientaux," *Echos d' Orient*, 34 (1935) 128-38.

Dvornik, Francis. *The Idea of Apostolicity in Byzantium and the Legend of the Apostle Andrew*. Cambridge, MA., 1958

Dvornik, Francis. *The Photian Schism, History and Legend*. Cambridge, 1948.

Ebersolt, J. *Constantinople byzantine et les voyageurs au Levant*. Paris, 1918.

Emilianides, A. *Histoire de Chypre*. Paris, 1963.

Enlart, E. *L' Art gothique et la renaissance en Chypre*. 2 vols. Paris, 1899.

Evodokimov, Paul. "Les principaux courantes de l' ecclésiologie Orthodoxe au XIXe siècle." *L' Ecclésiologie au XIXe siècle*. Paris, 1960, pp. 57-76.

Fabre, P. and Duchesne, L. *Le Liber Censum de l' Eglise Romaine.* Paris, 1901-10.

Faral, E. "Geoffrey de Villehardouin, La question de sa sincerité," *Revue Historique,* 178 (1936) 530-82.

Folz, Robert. *L' Idée d' Empire en Occident du Ve au XIVe siècle.* Paris, 1953.

Fotheringham, J. "Genoa and the Fourth Crusade," *English Historical Review,* 25 (1910) 20-57.

Fournier, Paul. "Les Conflits de juridiction entre l' église et le pouvoir seculier de 1180 à 1328," *Revue des questions historiques,* 27 (1880) 432-64.

Fournier, Paul and Le Bras, Gavriel. *Histoire des Collections Canoniques en Occident depuis les fousses decretales jusqu' au Décret de Gratien.* 2 vols. Paris, 1931-32.

Freeman, Ann. "Further Studies in the *Libri Carolini III.* The Marginal Notes in *Vaticanus Latinus 7207,*" *Speculum,* 46 (1971) 597-612.

Frolow, A. "La dedicace de Constantinople dans la tradition byzantine." *Revue de l' histoire de religions.* Paris, 1944, pp. 61 ff.

Frolow, A. "La déviation de la IVe Croisade vers Constantinople. Problème d' histoire et de doctrine," *Revue de l' histoire des religious.* 144 (1954) 168-87 (Part 1); 146 (1955) 67-128 (Part 2) and pp. 194-219 (Part 3). Published as *Recherches sur la déviation de la IVe Croisade vers Constantinople.* Paris, 1955.

Galavaris, George. *Bread and the Liturgy: The Symbolism of Early Christian and Byzantine Bread Stamps.* Wisconsin, 1970.

Gardner, A. *The Lascarids of Nicaea, The Story of an Empire in Exile.* London, 1912.

Geanakoplos, Deno John. *Byzantine East and Latin West.* New York and Evanston, 1966.

Geanakoplos, Deno John. *Emperor Michael Paleologus and the West, 1258-1282.* Cambridge, MA., 1959

Geanakoplos, Deno John. "On the Schism of the Greek and Roman Churches: A Confidential Papal Directive for the Implementation of Union." *The Greek Orthodox Theological Review,* 1 (1954) 16-24.

Gill, Joseph. *The Council of Florence.* Cambridge, 1961.

Gill Joseph. "Filioque." *New Catholic Encyclopedia.* Vol. 5. New

York, 1966. Pp. 913-914.

Gregoire, H. "The Question of the Diversion of the Fourth Crusade." *Byzantion,* 15 (1940) 158-66.

Grousset, Rene. *L' empire du Levant — Histoire de la question d' Orient au moyen âge.* Paris, 1946.

Grousset, Rene. *Histoire des Croisades et du royaume franc de Jérusalem.* 3 vols. Paris, 1934-36.

Grumel, F. "Les Preliminaires du schisme de Michel Cerulaire ou la question romaine avant 1054." *Revue des études byzantines.* 10 (1952) 5-23.

Grumel, V. "Y' eut-el un second schisme de Photius." *Revue des Sciences, Philosophique et Theologique.* 12 (1933) 432-57.

Guerdan, Rene. *Byzantium.* New York, 1957.

Gunnis, R. *Historic Cyprus.* London, 1936.

Gursch, M.R. "A Twelfth Century Preacher-Fulk of Neuilly." *The Crusades.* Ed. Paetow. New York, 1938. pp. 183-206.

Hackett, J. *A History of the Orthodox Church of Cyprus.* London, 1901.

Hammer, William. "The Concept of the New or Second Rome in the Middle Âges." *Speculum,* 19 (1945) 1-42.

Hanotaux, Gabriel. "Les Venitiens ont-ils trahi la Chrétienté en 1202?" *Revue Historique,* 4 (1877) 74-102.

Hazlitt, Carew W. *The Venetian Republic, its Rise, its Growth, and its Fall.* 2 vols. London, 1915. Reprinted in New York. Ams. Press, Inc., 1966. Vol. 1.

Hill, G. *History of Cyprus.* 4 vols. Cambridge, 1949-1952.

Hill, J.H. "Raymond of St. Giles in Urban's Plan of Greek and Latin Friendship." *Speculum,* 24 (1951) 265-76.

Hill, J.H. and Hill, Laurita L. "The Convention of Alexius Comnenus and Raymond of St. Giles," *American Historical Review,* 58 (1952-53) 322-27.

Huizing, Peter. "The Earliest Development of Excommunication *Latae Sententiae* by Gratian and the Decretists," *Studia Gratiana,* 3 (1955) 279-320.

Hulphen, F.C. "Le rôle des 'Latins' dans l' histoire interieure de Constantinople à la fin du XIIe siècle," *Melanges pour Ch. Diehl. 1 (Paris, 1930) 141-45.*

Hussey, Joan. *The Byzantine World.* London, 1957.

Janin, R. "Les Francs au service des 'Byzantins'," *Echos d' Orient,* 29 (1930) 61-72.

Janin, R. "Au lendemain de la conquête de Constantinople. Les tentatives d' union des Eglises, 1204-1214," *Echos d' Orient,* 32 (1933) 5-21, 195-202.

Jenkins, Romilly. *Byzantium: The Imperial Centuries, A.D. 610-1071.* London, 1966, and New York, 1970.

Joranson, Einar. "The Alleged Frankish Protectorate in Palestine," *American Historical Review,* 33 (1927) 241-61.

Joranson, Einar. "The Problem of the Spurious Letter of Emperor Alexius to the Count of Flanders," *American Historical Review,* 55 (1950) 811-32.

Jorga, N. *Histoire de la vie byzantine.* 3 vols. Bucharest, 1934.

Jorga, N. *Notes et extraits pour servir à l' histoire des Croisades au XVe siècle.* 6e ser. 6 vols. Paris and Bucharest, 1899-1916.

Jugie, M. *Le schisme byzantin.* Paris, 1941.

Kantorowicz, Ernest H. *The King's Two Bodies: A Study in Medieval Political Theology.* Princeton, 1957.

Kohler, C. "Documents Chypriotes du debut de XIVe siècle," *Rev. Or. Lat.,* 11 (1905-08) 440-52.

Kuttner, Stephan. "A Collection of Decretal Letters of Innocent III in Bamberg," *Medievalia et Humanistica.* New Series. 1 (1970) 41-56.

Kuttner, Stephan. *Harmony from Dissonance/ An Interpreation of Medieval Canon Law.* Latrobe, PA, 1960.

Ladner, G. "The Concepts of 'Ecclesia' and 'Christianitas' and Their Relation to the Idea of Papal 'Plenitudo Potestatis' from Gregory VII to Boniface VIII," *Miscellanea historiae Pontificiae,* 18 (1954) 39-77.

LaMonte, John L. *Feudal Monarchy in the Latin Kingdom of Jerusalem.* Cambridge, MA, 1932.

LaMonte, John L. "The Lords of Caesarea in the Period of the Crusades," *Speculum,* 22 (1947) 145-61.

LaMonte, John L. "The Lords of Sidon in the Twelfth and Thirteenth Centuries," *Byzantion,* 17 (1944-45) 183-211.

LaMonte, John L. "The Rise and Decline of the Frankish

Seigneury in the Time of the Crusades," *Revue Historique sud-est Européène,* 15 (1938) 301-20.

LaMonte, John L. "The Significance of the Crusaders' States in Medieval History," *Byzantion,* 15 (1940) 300-15.

LaMonte, John L. "Some Problems in European Crusading Historiography." *Speculum,* 15 (1940) 57-75.

LaMonte, John L. "Three Questions Concerning the Assizes of Jerusalem." *Byzantina-Metabyzantina.* 1,1 (1946) 201-11.

Lang, R.H. *Cyprus, Its History, Its Present Resources and Future Prospects.* London, 1878.

Langer, William L. "The Next Assignment." *American Historical Review.* 63 (1958) 203-304.

Lascaris, M. "Les Vlachorynchines une mise à point," *Revue Historique du Sud-est Européène,* 15 (1943) 182-189.

Laurent, V. "La Croisade et la question d' orient sous le pontificat de Gregoire X," *Revue Historique du Sud-est Européèn,* 22 (1945) 106-37.

Laurent, V. "Les fastes Episcopaux de l' Eglise de Chypre," *Etudes Byzantines,* 6 (1948) 153-69.

Laurent, V. "Les Manuscrits de l' histoire byzantine de Georges Pachymère," *Byzantion,* 5 (1929) 129 ff.

Laurent, V. "Notes de chronographie et d' histoire byzantine," *Echos d' Orient,* 36 (1937) 157-62.

Laurent, V. "Rome et Byzance sous le pontificat de Celestin III (1191-1198)," *Echos d' Orient,* 39 (1940) 26-58.

Lefevre, M. Yves. "Innocent IIIe et son temps vus de Rome. Etude sur la biographie anonyme de ce pape," *Melanges d' archeologie et d' histoire,* 59 (1949) 242-45.

Leib, Bernard. "Deux inédits byzantins (XIIe's) sur les azymes," *Orientalia Christiana,* Rome, 1924. Fasc. 9.

Lewis, Ewart. *Medieval Political Ideas.* 2 vols. New York, 1954.

Longnon, J. "Domination franque et civilisation grecque," *Melanges pour Ch. Picard,* 2 (1949) 659-67.

Longnon, J. *L' Empire Latin de Constantinople et la principauté de Morée.* Paris, 1949.

Longnon, J. ed. *Livre de la conquête de la princie de l' Amorée Chronique de Moréa (1204-1305).* Paris, 1911.

Longnon, J. "Problemes de l' histoire de la principauté de Morée," *Journal des Savants,* (1946) 73-93, 147-61.

Longnon, J. "Le rattachement de la principauté de Morée au royaume de Sicile en 1267," *Journale de Savants.* Paris, 1942.

Luchaire, A. *Innocent III.* 6 vols. Paris, 1905-08.

Luke, H. *Cyprus.* London, 1957.

Magoulias, Harry J. *Byzantine Christianity: Emperor, Church and the West.* Chicago, 1970.

Magoulias, Harry J. "A Study in Roman Catholic and Greek Orthodox Church Relations on the Island of Cyprus between the Years A.D. 1196 and 1360," *The Greek Orthodox Theological Review,* 10 (1964) 75-106.

Mallock, W.H. *In an Enchanted Island.* London, 1889.

Mann, Horace K. *The Lives of the Popes in the Middle Ages.* 18 Vols. London, 1902-1932.

Mas Latrie, L. de. "Archévêques latins de l' ile de Chypre." *Archives de l' Orient latin,* 2,1. 207-328.

Mas Latrie, L. de. *Généalogie des Rois de Chypre de la famille de Lusignan* (estrait de l' *Archivia Veneta).* Venice, 1881.

Mas Latrie, L. de. *Histoire de l' île de Chypre sous le vigne des princes de la maison de Lusignan.* 3 vols. Paris, 1855-61.

Mas Latrie, L. de. "Les Patriarches latins de Constantinople," *Rev. Or. Lat,* 3 (1895) 433-56.

McIlwain, Charles H. *The Growth of Political Thought in the West.* New York, 1932.

McNeal, E. "The Story of Isaac and Andronicus," *Speculum,* 9 (1934) 319-36.

Meyendorff, John. *Orthodoxy and Catholicity.* New York, 1966.

Meyendorff, J. "St. Peter in Byzantine Theology," *St. Vladimir's Seminary Quarterly Review,* 4 (1960) 26-48.

Michaud, Joseph Francis. *The History of the Crusades.* 3 vols. New York, n.d.

Miller, William. *Essays on the Latin Orient.* Cambridge, 1921.

Miller, William. "The Last Athenian Historian — Laonikos Chalkokondylas," *The Journal of Hellenic Studies,* 42 (1922) 36-49.

Miller, William. *The Latins in the Levant, A History of Frankish Greece (1204-1566)* London, 1908.

Milligen, A.Van. *Byzantine Constantinople — The Walls of the City and Adjoining Historical Sites.* London, 1899.

Munro, D.C. "A Crusader — Foucher de Chartres," *Speculum,* 7 (1932) 321-335.

Munro, D.C. "Did the Emperor Alexis I Ask for Aid at the Council of Piacenza?" *American Historical Review,* 27 (1922) 731-33.

Munro, D.C. *The Kingdom of the Crusaders.* New York, 1935.

Munro, D.C. "The Speech of Pope Urban II at Clermont," *American Historical Review,* 40 (1906) 231-42.

Muralt, Edouard de. *Essai de chronographie byzantine (1057-1453).* Basil and Geneva, 1871.

Murray, Alexander. "Pope Gregory VII and His Letters," *Traditio,* 22 (1966) 149-202.

Ostrogorsky, G. "Agrarian Conditions in the Byzantine Empire in the Middle Age," *Cambridge Economic History,* 1 (1941) 194-223.

Ostrogorsky, G. "Byzantine Cities in the Early Middle Ages," *Dumbarton Oaks Papers,* 13 (1959) 47-66.

Papadopoulos-Kerameus, A. "Documents grecs pour servir à l' histoire de la Quatriéme Croisade (Liturgie et reliques)," *Revue de l' Orient latin,* 6 (1898) 540-55.

Pears, E. *The Fall of Constantinople, Being the Story of the Fourth Crusade.* New York, 1886.

Pissard, H. *La guerre sainte en pays chrétien.* Paris, 1912.

Powell, James M., ed. *Innocent III, Vicar of Christ or Lord of the World.* Boston, 1963.

Prawer, J. "Etude de quelques problèmes agraires et sociaux d' une seigneurie croisee du XIIIᵉ siècle," *Byzantion,* 22 (1952) 5-61; 23 (1953) 143-70.

Queller, Donald E. "Innocent III and the Crusader-Venetian Treaty of 1201," *Medievalia et Humanistica,* 15 (1963) 32-47.

Riant, P. "Le changement de direction de la quatrième croisade d' aprés quelques travaux récents," *Revue des questions historiques,* 23 (1878) 71-114.

Riant, P. "Innocent III, Philippe de Souabe et Boniface de Mont-férrat," *Revue des questions historiques,* 17 (1875) 321-75; 18, 5-75.

Richard, J. "Pairie d' Orient Latin, les quatre baronnies des royaumes de Jerusalem et de Chypre," *Revue historique de Droit*

Francais et Etranger, 28 (1950) 67-68.

Rodd, Rennell J. *The Princes of Achaia and the Chronicles of the Morea, A Study of Greece in the Middle Ages.* 2 vols. London, 1907.

Runciman, S. "The Byzantine 'Protectorate' in the Holy Land," *Byzantion,* 18 (1948) 207-15.

Runciman, S. "The Decline of the Crusading Ideal," *Sewanee Review,* 79 (1971) 498-513.

Runciman, S. *The Great Church in Captivity.* Cambridge, 1968.

Runciman, S. *A History of the Crusades.* 3 vols. Cambridge, 1951-1954.

Runciman, S. *A History of the First Bulgarian Empire.* London, 1930.

Sacerdoteanu, A. "Considerations sur l[a] histoire des Roumains au Moyen-Age," *Melanges de l' Ecole Roumaine en France,* Paris, 1928. 103-245.

Sathas, C.N. *Bibliotheca Graeca Medii Aevi.* 7 vols. Venice and Paris, 1872-1894.

Sathas, C.N., ed. *Documents inédits relatifs a l' histoire de la Grèce au moyen âge.* 9 vols. Paris, 1880-1890.

Schaeffer, C.F.A. *Missions en Chypre, 1932-1935.* Paris, 1936.

Setton, Kenneth M. "Athens in the Later Twelfth Century," *Speculum,* 19 (1944) 179-207.

Setton, Kenneth M. general ed. *A History of the Crusades. I: The First Hundred Years.* Ed. M. W. Baldwin. 2nd ed. Madison, WI, 1969. *II: The Later Crusades, 1189-1311.* Ed. by R.L. Wolff and H. W. Hazard. 2nd ed. Madison, WI, 1969.

Sherrard, P. *The Greek East and the Latin West, A Study in the Christian Tradition.* Oxford, 1959.

Siadbei, L. "Sur les plus anciens sources de l' histoire des Roumains," *Annuaire de l' Institut de Philologie et d' Histoire orientales,* 2, Paris, 1934.

Spiteris, Tony. *The Art of Cyprus.* New York, 1970.

Stevenson, W.B. *The Crusaders in the East.* Cambridge, 1907.

Stewart, B. *Cyprus — The People, Medieval Cities, Castles, Antiquities and History of the Island.* London, 1908.

Storrs, R. *A Chronology of Cyprus.* Nicosia, 1930.

Storrs, R. and O' Brien, B. J. *Handbook of Cyprus.* New York, 1930.

Stubbs, W. "The Medieval Kingdoms of Cyprus and Armenia." *Seventeen Lectures on the Study of Medieval and Modern History and Kindred Subjects.* Chap. 8. 3rd ed. Oxford, 1900.

Tessier, Jules. *La Quatriéme Croisade—La diversion sur Zara et Constantinople.* Paris, 1884.

Thiriet, F. "Les chroniques venitiennes de la Marcienne et leur importance pour l' histoire de la romaine greco-venitienne," *Mélanges archéologiques et historiques,* 66 (1954) 241-92.

Throop, Palmer A. "Criticism of Papal Crusade Policy in' Old French and Provencal," *Speculum,* 13 (1938) 379-412.

Throop, Palmer A. *Criticism of the Crusade — A Study of Public Opinion and the Crusade Propaganda.* Amsterdam, 1940.

Tierney, Brian. "The Continuity of Papal Political Theory in the Thirteenth Century. Some Methodological Considerations," *Medieval Studies,* 27 (1965) 227-45.

Tierney, Brian. "Some Recent Works on the Political Theories of the Medieval Canonists," *Traditio,* 10 (1952) 594-652.

Topping, Peter W. "The Formation of the Assizes of Romania," *Byantion,* 17 (1944-45) 304-19.

Topping, Peter W. *Feudal Institutions as Revealed in the Assizes of Romania.* Philadelphia, 1949.

Ullmann, W. *The Growth of Papal Government in the Middle Ages.* London, 1955.

Ullman, W. "A Medieval Document on Papal Theories of Government," *English Historical Review,* 61 (1946) 180-201.

Ullmann, W. *Medieval Papalism: The Political Theories of the Medieval Canonists.* London, 1949.

Vasiliev, A. "The Foundation of the Empire of Trebizond 1204-1222," *Speculum,* 10 (1936) 1-37.

Vasiliev, A. *History of the Byzantine Empire (324-1453).* Madison, WI, 1952.

Vasiliev, A. "On the Question of Byzantine Feudalism," *Byzantion,* 8 (1933) 584-604.

Villey, M. *La Croisade. Essai sur la formation d' une théorie juridique.* Paris, 1942.

Waley, Daniel. *The Papal Stone in the Thirteenth Century.* London, 1961.

Watt, John A. "The Early Medieval Canonists and the Forma-
tion of Consiliar Theory," *Irish Theolgoical Quarterly*, 24 (1957) 13-31.
Watt, John A. *The Theory of Papal Monarchy in the Thirteenth
Century.* New York, 1965.
Wins, C. "Elogue historique de Boudoin de Constantinople,"
*Mémoires et publications de la société des scientes, des arts, et des
lettrés du Hainaut,* 2 series. Vol. 3. Belgium, 1856.
Wolff, Robert Lee. "Baldwin of Flanders and Hainaut, First Latin
Emperor of Constantinople: His Life, Death and Resurrection,
1172-1225," *Speculum,* 27 (1952) 281-322.
Wolff, Robert Lee. "Footnote to an Incident of the Latin Occupa-
tion of Constantinople: The Church and the Icon of the Hodegetria,"
Traditio, 6 (1948) 319-28.
Wolff, Robert Lee. "Mortage and Redemption of an Emperor's
Son: Castile and the Latin Empire of Constantinople," *Speculum,*
29 (1954) 45-84.
Wolff, Robert Lee. "The Organization of the Latin Patriarchate
of Constantinople, 1204-1261," *Traditio,* 6 (1948) 33-60.
Wolff, Robert Lee. "Romania: The Latin Empire of Constantino-
ple," *Speculum,* 23 (1948) 1-34.

F. Translations of Primary and Secondary Sources and Collections

Diehl, Charles. *Byzantium: Greatness and Decline.* Translated from
French by Naomi Walford. New Jersey, 1957.
Dubois, Pierre. *The Recovery of the Holy Land.* English transla-
tion from Latin with introduction and notes by Wolther Brandt. New
York, 1956.
Fra Angelo Calepio of Cyprus: Letters. Translated by Claude
Delavel Cobham. *Excerpta Cypria.* Cambridge, 1908. 122-162.
Gregorovius, F. *History of the City of Rome in the Middle Ages.*
("Geschichte der Stadt Rom in Mittelalter") English translation from
German by Annie Hamilton. 8 vols. in 13. London, 1894-1902.
Grousset, Rene. *The Epic of the Crusades.* Translated from French
by Noel Lindsay. New York, 1970.
Helmold (Helmoldus presbyter bosoviensis). *The Chronicle of the*

Slavs by Helmold, Priest of Bosau. English translation from Latin by F.J. Tschau. New York, 1935.

Hill, John Hugh, and Hill, Laurita L., eds. and trans. *Raymond d' Aguilers Historia Francorum qui ceperunt Iherusalem.* Philadelphia, 1968.

Hill, Rosalind M.T. and Mynors, Sir Rogers, eds. and trans. *Gesta Francorum et Aliorum Hierosulimitanorum.* London, 1962.

Joinville, Jean Sire de. *Chronicle (Histoire de Saint Louis, Credo, et Lettre a Louis X).* English translation by Sir Frank T. Marzials. New York, 1958. (French edition by N. de Wailly, with translation into Modern French. 1874.)

Karmires, John. "The Schism of the Roman Church." Translated from Greek by Z. Xintaras. Θεολογία, 21 (1950) 37-67.

The Liber Augustalis or the Constitutions of Melfi Promulgated by the Emperor Frederick II for the Kingdom of Sicily in 1231. Translated with introduction by James M. Powell. New York, 1971.

Makhairas, Leontios. *Recital Concerning the Sweet Land of Cyprus Entitled "Chronicle."* 2 vols. Greek text and English translated by R.M. Dawkins. Oxford, 1932. Greek text and French translation by E. Miller and C. Sathas. 2 vols. Paris, 1881-1882. Greek text. *Bibliotheca Graeca Medii Aevi.* Edited by C. Sathas. Vol. 2. Venice, 1873.

Mann, W.E. *The Lives of the Popes.* English translation by F.I. Antrobus and D.F. Kerr. *The History of the Popes from the Close of the Middle Ages.* 12 vols. St. Louis, Missouri, 1898-1912.

Norden, Walter. *Der vierte Kreuzzug im Rahmen der Beziehungen des Abendlandes zu Byzanz.* Berlin, 1898. English translation from German by Donald E. Queller, ed. *The Latin Conquest of Constantinople.* New York, 1971. Pp. 1-2, 11-27, 30-33, 35-36, 44-48.

Odo de Deuil. *De profectione Ludovici VII in Orientem.* Latin text and English translation by V.G. Berry. New York, 1948. (French ed. by H. Waquet. Paris, 1949.)

Ostrogorsky, G. *History of the Byzantine State.* Translation by Joan Hussey. Oxford, 1956.

Otto of Freising. *The Deeds of Frederick Barbarossa (Gesta Friderici I Imperatoris).* English translation by C.C. Mierow and R. Emory. New York, 1953.

Papaioannou, Charilaos. *History of the Orthodox Church in Cyprus.* J. Hackett. Vol. 1. Athens, 1923. Vol. 2. Peiraieus, 1927. Vol. 3. Peiraieus, 1932.

Philip of Novara. *The Wars of Frederick II Against the Ibelins in Syria and Cyprus, by Philip of Novara.* English translation from French version of Ch. Kohler, based on the two major sources: *Gestes des Chiprois* and *Chronicle of Amadi.* Notes and introduction by J.L. LaMonte, and verse translation by M.J. Hubert. New York, 1936.

Robert de Clari. *The Conquest of Constantinople.* ("La Conquête de Constantinople") English version from Old French by E.H. McNeal. New York, 1936. (French ed. by Laver. Paris, 1924.)

Ryan, Frances Rita, ed. and trans. *Fulcher of Chartres, A History of the Expedition to Jerusalem, 1095-1127.* Knoxville, Tennessee, 1969.

Vacalopoulos, Apostolos E. *Origins of the Greek Nations: The Byzantine Period, 1204-1461.* Trans. Ian Moles, revised by the author. New Brunswick, 1970.

Villehardouin, Geoffroy de. *De la conquête de Constantinople.* English version from Old French by Sir Frank T. Marzials. New York, 1958. (French ed. by N. de Wailly, 1872, 1874.)

Wibrandi de Oldenborg Peregrinatio. Published by J.C.M. Laurent. *Peregrinatores Medii Aevi Quator.* 2nd ed. Leipzig, 1873. Translated by Claude Delaval Cobham. *Excerpta Cypria.* Cambridge, 1908. 13-15.

William of Tyre. *A History of Deeds Done Beyond the Sea, by William, Archbishop of Tyre.* English translation from Latin by E.A. Babcock and A.C. Krey. 2 Vols. New York, 1943. (Text ed., *Historia Rerum in Partibus Transmarinis Gestarum. Recueil, Historiens Occidentaux.* Vol. 1. See Section A.)

Index

191

835—
Y18.19